Ask Billy Graham

ASK BILLY GRAHAM

COMPILED BY BILL ADLER

THOMAS NELSON
Since 1798

NASHVILLE   DALLAS   MEXICO CITY   RIO DE JANEIRO   BEIJING

Published in Nashville, Tennessee, by Thomas Nelson. Thomas Nelson is a trademark of Thomas Nelson, Inc.

Thomas Nelson, Inc. books may be purchased in bulk for educational, business, fund-raising, or sales promotional use. For information, please e-mail SpecialMarkets@ThomasNelson.com.

Library of Congress Cataloging-in-Publication Data
Walker, Jay, 1973-
  Ask Billy Graham / by Bill Adler.
     p. cm.
  Includes bibliographical references and index.
  ISBN: 978-0-8499-0310-6 (hardcover)
  ISBN: 978-0-8499-1982-4 (IE)
  1. Graham, Billy, 1918—Interviews. 2. Evangelists—United States—Interviews.
3. Christianity—20th century. 4. Theology. 5. World politics—20th century. 6. Moral conditions. I. Title.
  BV3785.G69W34 2007
  269'.2092—dc22

                                                                  2007015908

Printed in the United States of America
07 08 09 10 11 RRD 6 5 4 3 2 1

CONTENTS

INTRODUCTION

WOULD YOU LIKE TO KNOW WHAT BILLY GRAHAM THINKS about his life, his work, and his family? What about politics, presidents, terrorism?

This book contains answers to questions many of us would ask Billy Graham if we had the good fortune to sit down with the person who many call "America's pastor." Taken from his sermons, speeches, interviews, television appearances, and writings, Graham's personal thoughts on family, politics, evangelism, and his relationship with U.S. presidents are captured in an easy-to-follow, question-and-answer format. In *Ask Billy Graham*, this world-famous preacher tackles tough issues such as matters of faith, marriage, drug use, and our relationship with God. Some of his responses are to direct inquiries from reporters, interviewers, and his audience. Others are in reply to rhetorical questions Graham posed to himself in sermons. Still others are answers to age-old questions such as "What will heaven be like?" or "Why does God send natural disasters?" In this book, Graham covers it all.

Also included are special sections such as "A List of Crusades and Missions" and "A Partial List of Awards and Honors." Why a *partial* list of awards? Graham has received so many accolades in his life that nobody is certain that the list is complete!

But before reading his inspiring words and learning from his accumulated wisdom, take a minute to discover a little about the man we know as Billy Graham:

Billy Graham was born William Franklin Graham Jr. on November 7, 1918, near Charlotte, North Carolina, to dairy farmers William Franklin and Morrow Coffey Graham, who attended the Associate Reformed Presbyterian Church. Billy was the first of four children, followed by Catherine, Melvin, and Jean.

Graham grew up during the time of tent revival meetings and traveling evangelists. One of those who toured the South was evangelist Mordecai Ham, who came to Charlotte in 1934. One night, mainly out of curiosity, Graham attended one of Ham's meetings and was so moved by the sermon that he committed himself to Christ. He knew then that he wanted to live a Christian life and help others do the same.

Graham enrolled at Bob Jones College, a fundamentalist school in Cleveland, Tennessee. He soon dropped out, however, and transferred to Florida Bible Institute (now Trinity College) in January 1937. He graduated with a bachelor of theology in 1940 and then attended Wheaton College in Wheaton, Illinois. He graduated in 1943 with a bachelor of arts in anthropology. It was at Wheaton that he met his future wife, Ruth Bell, the daughter of missionaries who had been stationed in China. (Indeed, Ruth spent much of her own youth in the Far East.) The two were married after graduation.

Soon Graham began preaching on street corners and in rescue missions to anyone who would listen. Friends at the time reported that he would even preach in front of saloons, often at his own physical peril. He was undeterred. Graham was baptized in accordance with the Southern Baptist Convention, and the following year he was ordained as a Southern Baptist minister in the St. John's River Association.

Graham's career got a jump start when he became vice president of Youth for Christ, a group that evolved from spirited rallies held all over the country and aimed at young people. Graham traveled throughout North America and Europe, speaking at rallies and organizing chapters. Eventually, though, Graham began to organize his own evangelistic rallies, and in 1948 he resigned from Youth for Christ.

Graham's rallies featured solo vocalist George Beverly Shea, choir director and master of ceremonies Cliff Barrows, and associate evangelist Grady Wilson. These people became his lifelong friends and associates. Because of his robust rallies and energetic sermons, Graham's name soon became well known within the evangelistic community, making him a sought-after preacher.

In 1949, Graham received his big break. While leading a campaign in Los Angeles, Graham attracted the attention of newspaper publisher William Randolph Hearst, who ordered his reporters to "puff Graham," meaning that they were to write highly positive (some would say fawning) pieces about the preacher. Graham's L.A. campaign, originally scheduled for three weeks, lasted seven weeks, during which time he was in the national spotlight. His story appeared not only in the local papers but in Hearst's nationwide chain of newspapers. Awareness continued to grow as publisher Henry Luce printed articles about Graham in his large-circulation magazines, *Time* and *Life*.

Graham's momentum continued. He followed up his success in Los Angeles with rallies in Africa, Asia, South America, and Europe, including blockbuster rallies in London in 1954 and New York in 1957. He was fast becoming an American institution and an international phenomenon.

In 1950 he established the Billy Graham Evangelistic Association (BGEA) in Minneapolis and began preaching on the air, on his weekly radio show *Hour of Decision*. Soon he also began spreading the gospel on film through his company World Wide Pictures, which produced movies with Christian themes. Graham was a brilliant manager, running his organization much like a business. He avoided the scandals that plagued many other evangelists by refusing to keep donations for himself. Instead he was paid a reasonable salary from BGEA and made sure that his personal life was above reproach. (For example, Graham made the decision never to be alone with a woman who was not his wife—not even dinner in a public restaurant—no matter what the circumstance.)

By the late 1950s and early '60s, Graham was holding three to five crusades annually, and his popularity soared. He was also on television with a TV version of his *Hour of Decision* radio program. Graham then became a prolific writer and author, producing hundreds of magazine articles and scores of books, including several bestsellers such as his autobiography *Just as I Am*. Later, BGEA published *Decision* magazine. (See "The Billy Graham Evangelistic Association Fact Sheet" on page 132 for a listing of the group's projects and programs.)

One of Graham's greatest achievements was spreading the gospel through state-of-the-art technology. He astounded the world when his March 1995 Global Mission in Puerto Rico reached an estimated one billion people in 185 countries via television, videotape, and satellite. It was a landmark event and propelled Graham farther than any modern preacher had gone.

Graham also made his mark on politics, having known every president since Harry Truman, and becoming close friends with many of them, including Richard Nixon and Ronald Reagan. Through the years, Graham became the confidant of politicians and business scions who sought his counsel, and even participated in several White House and inaugural events. (See "Billy Graham's Participation in Inaugural Events and Ceremonies" on page 75.)

Now in his late eighties, Graham has probably preached his last crusade (now called "missions") because of ill health. But despite his infirmities, he continues to comfort us with TV appearances, articles, books, and columns. He was a source of great solace after the tragedy of 9/11, delivering a sermon so compelling and healing that it is included in its entirety in this book.

Although there will never be another Billy Graham, his words and deeds will live forever. Many of his works are available for academic study at Wheaton College's Billy Graham Center. Also, projected for completion in 2007, the $25 million Billy Graham Library will open in Charlotte, North Carolina, and will offer visitors exhibits, multimedia displays, and films to present the gospel and the life, ministry, and message of Billy Graham.

Now, sit back and read answers from the man who many Americans consider the most important religious figure of the twentieth century. The one whose simple message—"My one purpose in life is to help people find a personal relationship with God . . . through knowing Christ"—will undoubtedly leave a legacy unmatched by any modern preacher. You will find his words both inspiring and comforting.

On CELEBRITY

WHAT IS THE UPSIDE OF BEING FAMOUS?
"I have said hundreds of thousands of times, on the radio and television, please write to us, 'Billy Graham, Minneapolis, Minnesota.' Then I would say, 'That's all the address you need.' . . . But we've gotten letters here that said 'Billy Graham, Somewhere in the World.'"

— STAR TRIBUNE (MINNEAPOLIS, MN), JUNE 20, 1996

WHAT HAS BEEN THE DOWNSIDE OF BEING SO WELL KNOWN?
"We had the FBI come sometime in the middle 1950s when I was getting a lot of hate mail and a lot of threats. And they said you should have a fence around your place. We hated it. We found it also gave us a lot of privacy, which we have needed from time to time. It doesn't do much good, because anybody who wants to can come see us."

— CHATTANOOGA TIMES FREE PRESS (TENNESSEE), SEPTEMBER 28, 1996

WHO IS RESPONSIBLE FOR YOUR NOTORIETY?
"I think the media and the papers have put me on a pedestal I don't deserve to be on. I'm not a great preacher. I'm just an ordinary proclaimer of the Gospel."

— THE POST AND COURIER (CHARLESTON, SC), SEPTEMBER 25, 1996

WHAT WAS THE REAL MEANING OF THE STAR THAT YOU
RECEIVED IN HOLLYWOOD?
(To celebrate his fortieth anniversary in the ministry, he received a side-walk star on the Hollywood Walk of Fame. The star's placement, the last open spot in front of Mann's Chinese Theater, was much coveted by some stars who were passed over for this location.)
"This star today is not a mark to recognize a man, but a marking for the glory of God. What this star represents is the faithfulness of God. . . . I feel somewhat out of place because I'm not sure that a clergyman belongs here . . . I feel a little lonely out there."

—ASSOCIATED PRESS, OCTOBER 16, 1989;

LOS ANGELES TIMES, OCTOBER 16, 1989

AT FIRST YOU TURNED DOWN THE STAR ON THE HOLLYWOOD
WALK OF FAME, BUT YOU CHANGED YOUR MIND. WHY?
"A star was offered to me 30 years ago, and I said, 'no,' then. But I've changed my views. Some parents walking along there someday in the future might be asked by their child, 'Who was Billy Graham?' And they could say, 'He preached the Gospel.'"

—*LOS ANGELES TIMES*, OCTOBER 14, 1989

HOW DO YOU HANDLE COMPLETE STRANGERS COMING OVER
TO YOU IN RESTAURANTS?
"I go to different restaurants dressed in old clothes. I wear blue jeans, but people are beginning to recognize me, no matter how I'm dressed now. And they come up to us and talk, or I invite them over to the table to sit down and talk."

—*THE POST-STANDARD* (SYRACUSE, NY), APRIL 29, 1989

HOW DO YOU FEEL ABOUT PEOPLE EXALTING YOU?

"People shouldn't put me up on a pedestal. When I think about the times I failed the Lord, I feel this low [as the floor]. . . . I'm praying that this book [the Bible] will honor and glorify God, not me."

— *SOUTH BEND TRIBUNE* (INDIANA), MAY 5, 2003

HOW DO YOU FEEL ABOUT BEING CALLED "REVEREND" OR "DOCTOR"?

"I don't find anywhere in the Bible that anybody was called reverend except God. I never liked the term doctor, because I do not have an earned doctor's degree, and I have great respect for those who do."

— *THE SAN DIEGO UNION-TRIBUNE*, MAY 4, 2003

On THE CHURCH

DID YOU EVER WANT YOUR OWN CHURCH?

"I knew from the start that I was going to work with all churches. I didn't want to build my own church. When people come forward we urge them to go to the church of their choice."

— *STAR TRIBUNE* (MINNEAPOLIS, MN), MAY 17, 1996

HAS THE UNITED STATES LEANED TOO FAR IN ITS UNDERSTANDING OF THE SEPARATION OF CHURCH AND STATE?

"The Founding Fathers meant that there should be no state church, but we've separated the state from all religion."

— *HOUSTON CHRONICLE*, MAY 8, 1993

WHAT CAN BRING DIFFERENT SEGMENTS OF THE SOUTHERN BAPTIST CHURCH TOGETHER DESPITE THEIR DIFFERENCES ON SCRIPTURE INTERPRETATION?

(Reverend Graham's response to this question was voiced aloud at the Southeastern Baptist Theological Seminary during a discussion in which he refused to take sides in the fight between fundamentalist and moderate wings of the Southern Baptist church over whether the Bible is the unequivocal Word of God or subject to interpretation.)

"The primary thing for us as a church is evangelism. You have a man [Lewis Drummond, then president of Southeastern Baptist

Theological Seminary] who knows how to teach it and set an example as president. He has a tremendous vision to train teachers, pastors, missionaries. Southeastern could become a beacon of light not only to the Southern Baptist Convention, but to all the world. . . . I don't get into Southern Baptist problems. I'm not getting into all the fighting. We can agree on one thing—and that is love."

—UNITED PRESS INTERNATIONAL, OCTOBER 12, 1988

DO YOU PLACE ANY IMPORTANCE ON A CHURCH'S
DENOMINATION OR LABEL?
"I have found in my travels across the world, that denominational or church labels actually have less importance than you might think. In fact, I have found that a strong and vibrant spiritual unity exists among all those who truly love Christ, and I have just as much fellowship with a believer in Russia or Singapore for example as I do closer to home."

—*DAILY TOWN TALK* (ALEXANDRIA, LA), DECEMBER 21, 2002

WHAT DID YOU MEAN WHEN YOU SAID THAT WHAT CHURCHES
NEEDED MOST WAS "REVIVAL AND RENEWAL"?
"The greatest burden we have is the need for revival and renewal within the churches. If the people within the churches are living as Christians are supposed to live and taking a stand on things they should be taking a stand on as a group, we could see a change in our country."

—PR NEWSWIRE, SEPTEMBER 30, 1993

BILLY GRAHAM'S
VOCATION FACT SHEET

1939   Ordained to the ministry by a church in the
Southern Baptist Convention

1943–45   Pastor, First Baptist Church, Western Springs, Ill.

1945–50   Charter Vice President, Youth for Christ
International, Chicago, Ill.

1947–52   President, Northwestern Schools, consisting of three
institutions: a liberal arts college, Bible school, and
theological seminary

1950   Founded Billy Graham Evangelistic Association,
Minneapolis, Minn.

1950   Began weekly *Hour of Decision* radio program, which
has been broadcast around the world on Sundays for
over fifty years

SOURCE: BILLY GRAHAM EVANGELISTIC ASSOCIATION

On COMPASSION

AT SOME TIME WE ALL FEEL OVERWHELMED BY ALL THE HURT
IN THE WORLD. HOW CAN WE HANDLE IT BETTER?
"Get involved. You can't heal every person. You can't feed every person. You can't give every person a home and a car. But you can help
some people. Visit those in the hospital and pray with them. If we all
do that, what a tremendous difference it would make."

— *AUSTIN AMERICAN-STATESMAN* (TEXAS), APRIL 4, 1997

WHAT CAN WE LEARN FROM JESUS ABOUT COMPASSION?
"Jesus never met a human need that He didn't supply. He made the
blind to see, the mute to speak, and the deaf to hear. He touched and
cleansed the lepers. He didn't just say, 'Be clean,' He touched them. He
got involved with them. Compassion means not only that you sit and
think how terrible that is, it means you get in step and try to help them."

— CRUSADE HELD AT SAN FRANCISCO'S COW PALACE,

OAKLAND POST, OCTOBER 19, 1997

HOW CAN WE BE MORE COMPASSIONATE?
"Look for ways to help other people. If somebody is sick, if somebody
is very old, we are to help. We are to be very kind and compassionate
and loving."

— *THE GUARDIAN* (LONDON), APRIL 19, 1988

IS THERE EVER ANY EXCUSE NOT TO HELP ALLEVIATE HUNGER AND POVERTY?

"This is part of our Christian responsibility and if rock stars can do it, how much more we, who call ourselves Christians, can do it." *(Referring to events such as the Live Aid concert to fight famine in Africa, and also announcing that his own group would contribute food overseas)*

—ASSOCIATED PRESS, JULY 20, 1985

HOW CAN WE LOVE OTHERS DESPITE OUR DIFFERENCES?

"You can't prove the existence of God. Nobody can prove his existence . . . I had to take that by faith. He wasn't the God of Abraham or the God of Billy Graham. He's the same God. He never changes. . . . The Bible says another thing about God: God is love, and he loves you tonight. . . . He can love through you and love people you don't like. That's an amazing thing. You may not like people of another race. You may not like people of another culture. But you can love them."

—*THE CINCINNATI ENQUIRER*, JUNE 30, 2002

AFTER HURRICANE KATRINA DEVASTATED NEW ORLEANS, YOU INVITED A FAMILY TO LIVE IN A SPARE HOME YOU OWN FOR SEVERAL MONTHS. WHAT SUGGESTION DID YOU OFFER AT THE TIME TO HELP THE REFUGEES FROM THIS NATURAL DISASTER?

"We knew that the money we had given was only a drop in the bucket compared to the need, and we began to feel burdened to invite a family that had lost everything to come and stay in the small house where we lived when we were first married. If every church in America adopted a family, it would solve the problem of how to house and help so many evacuees."

—*DESERET MORNING NEWS* (SALT LAKE CITY), SEPTEMBER 24, 2005

HOW DOES OUR RELATIONSHIP TO THE POOR AFFECT US?
"If we are blind to the suffering of others, then we have an even deeper blindness, a blindness of the spirit."

— *THE STUART NEWS/PORT ST. LUCIE NEWS* (STUART, FL), NOVEMBER 6, 1999

A List of Crusades and Missions
(IN ALPHABETICAL ORDER)

Aarhus, Denmark – *1955*
Aberdeen, Scotland – *1991*
Accra, Ghana – *1960*
Addis Ababa, Ethiopia – *1960*
Adelaide, Australia – *1959*
Albany, New York – *1990*
Albuquerque, New Mexico – *1952, 1975*
Altoona, Pennsylvania – *1949*
Amherst, Massachusetts – *1982 (University of Massachusetts)*
Amsterdam, The Netherlands – *1954*
Anaheim, California – *1969, 1985*
Anchorage, Alaska – *1984*
Arad, Romania – *1985*
Asheville, North Carolina – *1953, 1977*
Atlanta, Georgia – *1950, 1973, 1994*
Auburn, Alabama – *1965 (Auburn University)*
Auckland, New Zealand – *1959, 1969*
Augusta, Georgia – *1948*

Baltimore, Maryland – *1949, 1981*
Bangor, Maine – *1964*
Basel, Switzerland – *1960*
Baton Rouge, Louisiana – *1970*
Beijing, People's Republic of China — *1988, 1994*
Belfast, Ireland – *1961*

Berlin (GDR) – *1982*
Berlin, West Germany – *1954, 1960, 1966, 1990*
Bern, Switzerland – *1960*
Billings, Montana – *1987*
Birmingham, Alabama – *1964, 1972*
Birmingham, England – *1984*
Blackpool, England – *1982*
Boca Raton, Florida – *1961, 1981*
Boise, Idaho – *1982*
Boston, Massachusetts – *1950, 1964, 1982*
Boston, Massachusetts – *1982 (Northeastern University)*
Bradenton-Sarasota, Florida – *1961*
Bratislava, Czechoslovakia – *1982*
Brazzaville, Congo – *1960*
Brisbane, Australia – *1959, 1968*
Bristol, England – *1984*
Brno, Czechoslovakia – *1982*
Brussels, Belgium – *1975*
Bucharest, Romania – *1985*
Budapest, Hungary – *1985, 1989*
Buenos Aires, Argentina – *1962, 1991*
Buffalo, New York – *1988*
Bulawayo, South Rhodesia – *1960*
Burlington, Vermont – *1982*

Cairo, Egypt – *1960*
Calgary, Alberta, Canada – *1981*
Cambridge, England – *1980*
Cambridge, Massachusetts – *1982 (Harvard University –*
    JFK School of Government Memorial Chapel and *Massachusetts*
    Institute of Technology)

Canberra, Launceston and Hobart, Australia – *1959*
Cape Canaveral, Florida – *1961*
Chapel Hill, North Carolina – *1982*
Charlotte, North Carolina – *1947, 1958, 1972, 1996*
Chattanooga, Tennessee – *1953*
Cheyenne, Wyoming – *1987*
Chicago, Illinois – *1962, 1971*
Christchurch, New Zealand – *1959*
Cincinnati, Ohio – *1951, 1977, 2002*
Clearwater, Florida – *1961*
Cleveland, Ohio – *1972, 1994*
Cluj-Napoca, Romania – *1985*
Columbia, South Carolina – *1950, 1987*
Columbus, Ohio – *1964, 1993*
Copenhagen, Denmark – *1954, 1965*

Dallas, Texas – *1953*
Dallas/Fort Worth, Texas – *1971, 2002*
Denver, Colorado – *1965, 1987*
Detroit, Michigan – *1953, 1976*
Dortmund, West Germany – *1955, 1970*
Dothan, Alabama – *1965*
Douai, France – *1963*
Dresden (Saxony) (GDR) – *1982*
Dunedin, New Zealand – *1969*
Durban, South Africa – *1973*
Dusseldorf, West Germany – *1954*

East Rutherford, New Jersey – *1991*
Edinburgh, Scotland – *1991*
Edmonton, Alberta, Canada – *1980*

El Paso, Texas – *1962*
Enugu, Nigeria – *1960*
Essen, West Germany – *1960*
Essen, Germany – *1993*

Fargo, North Dakota – *1987*
Fort Lauderdale, Florida – *1961, 1985*
Fort Worth, Texas – *1951*
Fort Worth/Dallas, Texas – *1971, 2002*
Frankfurt, West Germany – *1954, 1955*
Fresno, California – *1958, 1962, 2001*
Fukuoka, Japan – *1980*

Gainesville, Florida – *1961*
Geneva, Switzerland – *1955*
Glasgow, Scotland – *1955, 1961, 1991*
Gorlitz (GDR) – *1982*
Gothenburg, Sweden – *1955, 1977*
Grand Rapids, Michigan – *1947*
Great Britain – *1967, 1989*
Greensboro, North Carolina – *1951*
Greenville, South Carolina – *1966*
Guangzhou, People's Republic of China – *1988*
Halifax, Nova Scotia, Canada –*1979*
Hamburg, West Germany – *1960*
Hamilton, Ontario, Canada – *1988*
Hanover, New Hampshire – *1982 (Dartmouth College)*
Hartford, Connecticut – *1982, 1985*
Helsinki, Finland – *1954, 1987*
Hilo, Hawaii – *1965*
Hollywood, California – *1951*

Hong Kong – *1975, 1990*
Honolulu, Oahu, Hawaii – *1965*
Houston, Texas – *1952, 1965, 1981*
Hyaiyin, People's Republic of China – *1988*

Ibadan, Nigeria – *1960*
Indianapolis, Indiana – *1959, 1980, 1999*
Ipswich, England – *1984*

Jackson, Mississippi – *1952, 1975*
Jacksonville, Florida – *1961, 2000*
Jacksonville, North Carolina – *1962*
Jerusalem, Jordan – *1960*
Johannesburg, South Africa – *1973*
Jos, Nigeria – *1960*

Kaduna, Nigeria – *1960*
Kahului, Maui, Hawaii – *1965*
Kansas City, Missouri – *1967, 1978*
Kiev, Ukraine, U.S.S.R. – *1988*
Kisumu, Kenya – *1960*
Kitwe, North Rhodesia – *1960*
Knoxville, Tennessee – *1970*
Kohima, Nagaland, India – *1972*
Kumasi, Ghana – *1960*

Lagos, Nigeria – *1960*
Las Vegas, Nevada – *1978, 1980*
Lausanne, Switzerland – *1960*
Leningrad, Russia, U.S.S.R. – *1984*
Lexington, Kentucky – *1971*

Lihue, Kauai, Hawaii – *1965*
Little Rock, Arkansas – *1959, 1989*
Livelink Centers, Great Britain – *1967, 1989*
Liverpool, England – *1984*
London, England – *1954, 1955, 1966, 1967, 1989*
Los Angeles, California – *1949, 1958, 1963*
Los Angeles, California – *1974 (25th Anniversary Celebration)*
Louisville, Kentucky – *1956, 1964, 2001*
Lubbock, Texas – *1975*
Lyon, France – *1963*

Manchester, England – *1961*
Manchester, New Hampshire – *1964, 1982*
Manila, Philippines – *1977*
Mannheim, West Germany – *1955*
Melbourne, Australia – *1959, 1969*
Memphis, Tennessee – *1951, 1978*
Mexico City, Mexico – *1981*
Miami, Florida – *1949, 1961*
Milwaukee, Wisconsin – *1979*
Minneapolis, Minnesota – *1950*
Minneapolis/St. Paul, Minnesota – *1961, 1973, 1996*
Modesto, California – *1948*
Monrovia, Liberia – *1960*
Montauban, France – *1963*
Montgomery, Alabama – *1965*
Montreal, Quebec, Canada – *1990*
Moscow, Russia, U.S.S.R. – *1982, 1984, 1988*
Moscow, Russia – *1992*
Moshi, Tanganyika – *1960*
Mulhouse, France – *1963*

Nairobi, Kenya – *1960, 1976*
Nancy, France – *1963*
Nanjing, People's Republic of China – *1988*
Nashville, Tennessee – *1954, 1979, 2000*
Nassau, Bahamas – *1982*
New Haven, Connecticut – *1982*
New Haven, Connecticut – *1982 (Yale University)*
New Orleans, Louisiana – *1954*
New Orleans, Louisiana – *1982 (Southern Baptist Convention Evangelistic Rally)*
New York City, New York – *1957, 1969, 1970, 1991, 2005*
New York City, New York – *1960 (Spanish)*
Newton, Massachusetts – *1982 (Boston College)*
Norfolk-Hampton, Virginia – *1974*
Norwich, England – *1984*
Novosibirsk, Siberia, U.S.S.R. – *1984*
Nurnberg, West Germany – *1955, 1963*

Oakland, California – *1971, 1997*
Okinawa, Japan – *1980*
Oklahoma City, Oklahoma – *1956, 1983, 2003*
Omaha, Nebraska – *1964*
Oradea, Romania – *1985*
Orlando, Florida – *1961, 1983*
Osaka, Japan – *1980*
Oslo, Norway – *1955, 1978*
Ottawa, Ontario, Canada – *1998*
Oxford, England – *1980*

Paris, France – *1954, 1955, 1963, 1986*
Peace River, Florida – *1961 (Sunrise Service)*

Pecs, Hungary – *1985*
Perth, Australia – *1959*
Philadelphia, Pennsylvania – *1961, 1992*
Phoenix, Arizona – *1964, 1974*
Pittsburgh, Pennsylvania – *1952, 1968, 1993*
Poland – *1978*
Ponce, Puerto Rico – *1967*
Portland, Maine – *1964, 1982*
Portland, Oregon – *1950, 1968, 1992*
Prague, Czechoslovakia – *1982*
Providence, Rhode Island – *1964, 1982*
Pyongyang, Korea (North) – *1992, 1994*
Raleigh, North Carolina – *1951, 1962, 1973*
Redstone Arsenal, Alabama – *1962*
Reno, Nevada – *1980*
Richmond, Virginia – *1956*
Rio de Janeiro, Brazil – *1960, 1974*
Rochester, New York – *1988*
Rotterdam, The Netherlands – *1955*

Sacramento, California – *1958, 1983, 1995*
Salisbury, Rhodesia – *1960*
San Antonio, Texas – *1958, 1968, 1997*
San Diego, California – *1958, 1964, 1976, 2003*
San Francisco, California – *1958, 1997*
San Jose, California – *1981, 1997*
San Juan, Puerto Rico – *1967, 1995*
Santa Barbara, California – *1958*
Sao Paulo, Brazil – *1979*
Satellite Locations in Iceland – *1978*
Satellite Locations in Norway – *1978*

Satellite Locations in Sweden – *1978*

Seattle, Washington – *1951, 1962, 1965, 1976, 1991*

Seoul, Korea (South) – *1973, 1984*

Shanghai, People's Republic of China – *1988*

Sheffield, England – *1985*

Shreveport, Louisiana – *1951*

Sibiu, Romania – *1985*

Singapore – *1978*

Sioux Falls, South Dakota – *1987*

South Bend, Indiana – *1977*

South Hamilton, Massachusetts – *1982 (Gordon-Conwell Seminary)*

Spokane, Washington – *1982*

Springfield, Massachusetts – *1982*

St. Louis, Missouri – *1953, 1973, 1999*

St. Paul/Minneapolis, Minnesota – *1961, 1973, 1996*

St. Petersburg, Florida – *1961*

Stendal (GDR) – *1982*

Stralsund (GDR) – *1982*

Stockholm, Sweden – *1954, 1978*

Stuttgart, West Germany – *1955, 1963*

Suceava, Romania – *1985*

Sunderland, England – *1984*

Sydney, Australia – *1959, 1968, 1979*

Syracuse, New York – *1953, 1989*

Tacoma, Washington – *1983, 1991*

Taipei, Taiwan – *1975*

Tallahassee, Florida – *1961, 1986*

Tallinn, Estonia, U.S.S.R. – *1984*

Tampa, Florida – *1961, 1979, 1998*

Timisoara, Romania – *1985*
Tokyo, Japan – *1967, 1980, 1994*
Toronto, Ontario, Canada – *1955, 1967, 1978, 1995*
Toulouse, France – *1963*
Tour-American Cities (Apr/May) – *1952*
Tour-American Cities (Aug) – *1952*
Tour-Caribbean – *1958*
Tour-Florida Cities – *1953*
Tour-Hungary – *1977*
Tour-India and Far East – *1956*
Tour-India Good News Festivals – *1977*
Tour-New England States – *1950*
Tour-Poland – *1978*
Tour-Scotland Cities – *1955*
Tour-South America (Jan/Feb) – *1962*
Tour-South America (Sept/Oct) – *1962*
Tour-Southern States – *1951*
Tour-U.S. Service Bases–West Germany – *1955*
Tour-U.S. West Coast – *1954*
Tour-West Texas – *1953*
Turin, Italy – *1967*
Tuscaloosa, Alabama – *1965 (University of Alabama)*
Tuskegee Institute, Alabama – *1965*

Uniondale (Long Island), New York – *1990*
Usumbura, Ruanda-Urundi – *1960*

Vancouver, British Columbia, Canada – *1965, 1984*
Vero Beach, Florida – *1961*
Villahermosa, Mexico – *1981*

Washington, DC – *1952, 1960, 1986*
Wellington, New Zealand – *1959*
West Palm Beach, Florida – *1961*
Wheaton, Illinois – *1959, 1980*
Williamsburg, Virginia – *1976*
Winnipeg, Manitoba, Canada – *1967*
Wittenberg (GDR) – *1982*

Zagorsk, Russia, U.S.S.R. – *1988*
Zagreb, Yugoslavia – *1967*
Zurich, Switzerland – *1955, 1960*

SOURCE: BILLY GRAHAM EVANGELISTIC ASSOCIATION

On COUNTRIES
HE HAS VISITED

DURING THE EARLY 1980S, POLAND WAS EXPERIENCING POLITICAL TURMOIL, AND GRAHAM VISITED THAT COUNTRY DURING A EUROPEAN TRIP THAT INCLUDED VISITING SEVERAL OTHER NATIONS. POLAND WAS UNDERGOING SOME DRASTIC CHANGES. WHAT WAS YOUR IMPRESSION OF ITS PEOPLE?

"Poland is one of the most religious countries of the world. I thought and still think the church and state have worked out a plan of working together that was quite unique. . . . They mutually have respect for each other. And, of course, the church has quite a bit of freedom to preach the gospel. There were no restrictions so far as I could tell."

—ASSOCIATED PRESS, DECEMBER 16, 1980

WHAT WAS YOUR HOPE FOR JAPAN, A COUNTRY WITH ABOUT 1 PERCENT OF THE POPULATION SEEING THEMSELVES AS CHRISTIANS?

"I, like most Americans, stand in awe of Japanese technology. All this has happened in 35 years. But it is my prayer that Japan will become a spiritual superpower, because that is what the world needs."

—ASSOCIATED PRESS, OCTOBER 1, 1980

WHAT WAS THE SIGNIFICANCE OF THE MIDDLE EAST TO
RELIGION?

"History began in that area of the world and the Bible teaches it will
end there in a conflagration. Somewhere in time, the last conflagration will take place in the Middle East. It's the part of the world
where Adam and Eve and the human race began, and the Bible
teaches that history will come to a conclusion there. Not the end of
the earth, but the end of history as we know it. But no one can
prophesy when that will be."

—ASSOCIATED PRESS, JANUARY 22, 1980

DO YOU BELIEVE THAT YOUR TEACHINGS ARE APPLICABLE TO
ALL COUNTRIES AND THEIR POLITICAL SYSTEMS?

"I teach that Christ is coming again, but until he comes we're going
to have to live on the same planet with Marxist people, with
Buddhist people, with people of all persuasions. God called me to the
whole world to preach the gospel, not just to capitalist countries."

—ASSOCIATED PRESS, NOVEMBER 4, 1982

HOW DID YOU HANDLE PREACHING IN COMMUNIST
COUNTRIES WHERE RELIGIOUS FREEDOM WAS SOMETIMES
LINKED TO POLITICAL FREEDOM?

"My message in [East] Berlin was the same as the apostle Paul's
when he came to Corinth. He did not comment on all the political
and social problems of Corinth. He did not even discuss the problems which may have existed between church and state. My aim was
to proclaim the Gospel of Jesus Christ, both publicly and privately."

—*THE WASHINGTON POST*, OCTOBER 16, 1982

YOU WERE CRITICIZED BY SOME WHO SAID THAT YOU PAINTED
A MORE ROSY PICTURE OF RELIGIOUS FREEDOM IN THE SOVIET
UNION AFTER YOUR TRIP THERE. HOW DID YOU RESPOND?
"Freedom is relative. I don't have freedom in the United States to go
into a public school and preach the Gospel, nor is a student free in a
public school to pray, or a teacher free to read the Bible publicly to
the students. At the same time, we have a great degree of freedom for
which I am grateful."

— *THE NEW YORK TIMES*, MAY 18, 1982

WHAT ARE YOUR THOUGHTS ABOUT CANADA?
"We love Canada—anytime I see the Maple Leaf anywhere in the
world, my heart warms as much as when I see the Stars and Stripes."

— *THE HAMILTON SPECTATOR* (ONTARIO, CANADA), JUNE 26, 1998

"Canada is looked upon as a peace-loving country. It's also looked
upon as a country that doesn't get involved in other people's affairs
around the world as much as the country I come from. We seem to
have our people everywhere telling other people what to do."

— *CALGARY HERALD* (ALBERTA, CANADA), JUNE 24, 1998

WHAT WAS YOUR GOAL IN VISITING CHINA?
"We're not a missionary organization. Our goal is to nurture the
indigenous Christian population. We facilitate relationships, diplo-
macy and understanding. We connect Christians there with overseas
Chinese Christians."

— *SEATTLE POST-INTELLIGENCER*, OCTOBER 29, 1997

DO YOU CONSIDER YOURSELF A CITIZEN OF THE WORLD
BECAUSE OF THE NUMBER OF COUNTRIES THAT YOU'VE
VISITED?
"I consider myself a world citizen because I've been to 105 countries,
preaching. And I have gotten to know a little of the cultures of those
countries. . . . I love them and respect them, and they have a right to
their own beliefs and their own choices. I don't try to coerce people
into receiving or following Christ. They make up their own minds.
But they're welcome to our services. Many of them come out of
curiosity to see what it's like, just as, when I've gone to India, I've
attended many Hindu meetings. . . . And they have always welcomed
me very courteously, and that's the way I would welcome them to
come. They don't have to feel embarrassed or feel pounced upon to
be converted to Christianity. But of course, I would be happy to see
them get to know Christ and what Christ can do in their lives."

—*SAN JOSE MERCURY NEWS* (CALIFORNIA), SEPTEMBER 5, 1997

"I was born, bred and educated in America and I'm a loyal citizen of
America. But I also consider myself a member of the world community with responsibilities not only to one nation but to the whole
human race."

—UNITED PRESS INTERNATIONAL, MAY 8, 1982

DURING THE EARLY DAYS OF TRADE WITH CHINA, YOU
SUPPORTED INCREASING TIES TO THAT COUNTRY. WHY?
"China is rapidly becoming one of the dominant economic and polit-
ical powers in the world, and I believe it is far better for us to keep
China as a friend than to treat it as an adversary. In my experience,
nations respond to friendship just as much as people do."

—*THE CHARLOTTE OBSERVER* (NORTH CAROLINA), JUNE 29, 1997

HOW WERE YOU ABLE TO OBTAIN ACCESS TO CHINA EARLIER
THAN OTHER AMERICANS?
"That happened because we went to the Chinese government with
openness and friendship, not threats."

— *THE SEATTLE TIMES*, JUNE 23, 1997

HOW DO YOU SEPARATE A COUNTRY'S DISTASTEFUL POLITICAL
SYSTEM, SUCH AS NORTH KOREA, FROM THE PEOPLE WITHIN
WHO ARE NEEDY?
"Whether or not we agree with the DPRK's [Democratic People's
Republic of Korea] political system, those of us who are Christians
should not stand by and allow people to starve. Everywhere we went
we stressed that we were not acting for political reasons, but simply as
Christians wanting to express our love to others. Food should not be
used as a political weapon in the face of a potential human disaster."

— PR NEWSWIRE, JUNE 12, 1996

YOU'VE PREACHED THE SAME PHILOSOPHY BUT SOFTENED
YOUR VIEWS ON SOME ISSUES. HOW HAS YOUR STANCE ON
COMMUNISM CHANGED OVER THE YEARS?
From 1953: "Either communism must die or Christianity must die
because it's actually a battle between Christ and Anti-Christ."
From 1984: "We [the United States and Soviet Union] must learn to
coexist and even be friends."

— *THE CHARLOTTE OBSERVER* (NORTH CAROLINA), SEPTEMBER 24, 1996

ARE PEOPLE THE SAME THE WORLD OVER?
"There's been no change in the human heart, you see that over and
over again. What's going on in the Balkans or in Central Africa,
where I have three grandchildren working in Rwanda, has been going

on in other generations. Man's heart hasn't changed but neither has the Gospel."

— *THE TORONTO STAR*, JUNE 4, 1995

DO YOU FEEL THAT THE CHARGES AGAINST THE CHINESE GOVERNMENT OF HUMAN RIGHTS ABUSES AND PERSECUTING CHRISTIANS IN PARTICULAR WAS ACCURATE?

"Some of the human rights accusations are absolutely accurate and some that I have read, I think, are misinterpretations of each other's cultural backgrounds. We need to be very careful—and I would say to Christians, very prayerful—that we don't make accusations that we can't back up. . . . China is China. Two, or three or four hundred years is the way they [Chinese leaders] look at things. But we want them to do something overnight. We have to be patient . . . we are dealing with a culture that's the oldest continuous civilization in the world. You can't turn a country like that around on a dime as you can turn a ship in the Pacific."

— *SOUTH CHINA MORNING POST* (HONG KONG), FEBRUARY 4, 1994

YOU WERE THE FIRST FOREIGNER TO GIVE A SPEECH AT NORTH KOREA'S GREAT PEOPLE'S STUDY HOUSE, WHICH IS ROUGHLY EQUIVALENT TO THE LIBRARY OF CONGRESS IN THE UNITED STATES. THIS WAS DURING A TIME OF GREAT TENSION BETWEEN THE UNITED STATES AND THE DEMOCRATIC PEOPLE'S REPUBLIC OF KOREA. WHAT ROLE DID YOU SUGGEST CHRISTIANS CAN TAKE IN EASING THESE TENSIONS?

"When we come to know Christ by committing our lives to Him, God comes into our lives and begins to change us from within. And when we are changed from within, we become concerned about the problems of our world and we want to do something about them. . . . That is why I believe true religion has a legitimate place in modern society and why I believe Christ has a message for the people of North Korea. In my experience in many countries, Christians— although often a minority—make good citizens and have a positive effect on their societies."

—PR NEWSWIRE. FEBRUARY 3. 1994

HOW DID YOU CHALLENGE THE JAPANESE PEOPLE TO SPREAD THE GOSPEL?

"The church here has the authority, it has the message and it has the resources to touch all of the Asian Rim with the Gospel. You have businessmen all over the world selling Japanese products. You can do the same with the Gospel. Japanese ability, Japanese 'know-how' can take this message to the world. There is no greater export than the Gospel of Christ."

—CITING THE MISSION '94 CRUSADE IN TOKYO. *NEWS & RECORD* (GREENSBORO. NC). JANUARY 29. 1994

HOW DID YOU DESCRIBE NORTH KOREA AFTER YOUR VISIT THERE IN THE MID '90s?

"There hasn't been anything religiously in North Korea since the Communists took over. It's a very isolated country and may be the most isolated country in the world today. . . . They call him [North Korean President Kim Il Sung] 'The Great Leader.' There are statues of him all over the place. The people there really do love him. This is not a leader the people are ever going to overthrow in my judgment."

—ASSOCIATED PRESS. JUNE 28. 1994

WERE YOU CONCERNED ABOUT THE DELUGE OF AMERICAN
EVANGELISTS WHO ENTERED THE SOVIET UNION AFTER IT
COLLAPSED?
"I think there was a great deal of resentment . . . in the former Soviet
Union when so many Christian organizations rushed over there with-
out a proper study and a proper understanding of the situation. . . .
The new patriarch was very concerned because other groups came in
after we did, and he was afraid that they were not going to recognize
the value of the Orthodox church in the history of the Soviet Union
or the history of Russia. I have great respect for the Orthodox church.
I have great respect for the fact they have stood all these years."

— *PITTSBURGH POST-GAZETTE* (PENNSYLVANIA), JUNE 1, 1993

YOUR EARLY VISITS TO THE SOVIET UNION UNDER
COMMUNIST RULE WERE DICEY. WHAT DID YOU SAY TO THE
PEOPLE WHO CAME TO SEE YOU DESPITE POSSIBLE
RETRIBUTION FROM THE AUTHORITIES?
"I tried to tell them how hard it is to be a Christian. I didn't want
them to think it was easy. I told them it would be tough, that they
may be disowned by family, disowned by people. . . . There were no
gimmicks, no literature, no music during the invitation—simply the
shuffling of thousands of feet coming forward. It was like the Holy
Spirit came down in mighty power."

—ASSOCIATED PRESS, NOVEMBER 20, 1992

IN YOUR OPINION, WHAT KEPT EAST AND WEST GERMANY
TOGETHER EVEN WHEN THEY WERE SEPARATED BY THE COLD WAR?
"It is a sign of their vitality and their faithfulness that the one bond
between East and West Germany which was never completely sev-
ered during those almost 50 years of separation and atheistic rule in
the East was the fellowship of the churches." *(This query came during*

a weeklong visit to Germany where Graham met with German chancellor Helmut Kohl, addressed the Synod of the Protestant Church of Germany [EKD], and met with the country's highest-ranking Catholic bishop.)

—PR NEWSWIRE, NOVEMBER 5, 1992

WHAT HAS THE COLLAPSE OF THE SOVIET UNION MEANT FOR INTEREST IN RELIGION?

"The demise of communism has exposed a moral and spiritual vacuum and the need to find new foundations upon which to build the society here. People realize the past is gone, the future is uncertain and the present seems to be hopeless. As a result, many are open to God. . . . Here in Moscow, I find people are searching for something and so they are grabbing at anything. There is an emptiness in their hearts and a confusion in their minds due to the recent changes and they don't know where to turn. There is a struggle going on as to what they should put their faith in." *(This inquiry was posed during the Miracle in Moscow, a two-week crusade and visit to the Russian capital.)*

—PR NEWSWIRE, OCTOBER 26, 1992

WHAT WAS YOUR IMPRESSION OF NORTH KOREA?

"I've never seen anything like it. There is no crime, no unemployment. It is a very rich country with gold and other minerals. The capital is one of the most beautiful in the world." *(Graham made these observations during a trip in which he preached to about eight hundred people in two churches, one Protestant and one Catholic, in Pyongyang.)*

—*THE ATLANTA JOURNAL AND CONSTITUTION*, APRIL 9, 1992

WHAT WERE SOME OTHER IMPRESSIONS, MAINLY ABOUT RELIGION AND THE NORTH KOREAN PEOPLE?

"They live in a society which does not encourage religion and where it is not advantageous to be a Christian. They have much to teach those of us from other parts of the world about dedication and what it means to follow Jesus Christ regardless of the cost. . . . My prayer is that God will bless and strengthen the Christians of North Korea and that this trip might have made some contribution to peace in a complex and potentially dangerous part of East Asia."

—PR NEWSWIRE, APRIL 6, 1992

WHILE NOT DISCOUNTING PROBLEMS ALL OVER THE WORLD, ESPECIALLY THOSE IN THE MIDDLE EAST THAT ARE ACUTE, YOU SAID THAT AS A NATION, THE UNITED STATES SHOULD PAY CLOSE ATTENTION TO AREAS CLOSE TO HOME. WHAT DID YOU MEAN?
"My position is that we should pay far more attention to Latin America and Canada—the nations that are in our own hemisphere—than we spend in so many other parts of the world."

—PR NEWSWIRE, NOVEMBER 7, 1991

YOU WERE ECSTATIC AT THE TURNOUT AT YOUR HONG KONG CRUSADE IN 1990. WHAT DID YOU OUTLINE AS THE CHALLENGES AND TASKS FOR THAT REGION AT THE TIME, AS IT WAS PREPARING TO COME UNDER CHINA'S RULE IN 1997?
"In Hong Kong, you have a three-fold task: to conserve the past, to challenge the present and to chart the future. Your people are going to need help in the months ahead. . . . We've come to Hong Kong for one purpose—to proclaim the Gospel of Jesus Christ. The good news of the Gospel is that God loves you, God loves the people of China and God loves people all over the world."

—PR NEWSWIRE, NOVEMBER 19, 1990

WHY WERE YOU HESITANT ABOUT PREACHING IN BERLIN?
"They said they wanted a religious figure, someone well-known and accepted on both sides, to provide some Christian word on what has

happened. I told them I just didn't have the strength to do all that. I was determined to say 'no,' but after listening to the East Berliners tell me why I had to come, I had to give in, after all they've been through."

—*ARKANSAS DEMOCRAT-GAZETTE* (LITTLE ROCK), MARCH 10, 1990, WRITING ON AN EVANGELISTIC RALLY IN BERLIN, THE FIRST ECUMENICAL GATHERING OF EAST AND WEST GERMANS IN MORE THAN THIRTY YEARS

DURING THE VAST CHANGES IN EUROPE SIGNALED BY THE TEARING DOWN OF THE BERLIN WALL AND OTHER EVENTS, YOU WERE OPTIMISTICALLY CAUTIOUS ABOUT THE RELIGIOUS AND SPIRITUAL FUTURE OF THE REGION. WHY?

"The danger of nuclear confrontation has lessened but there are threats of hedonism, materialism and self-gratification. . . . A few weeks ago President (Vaclav) Havel of Czechoslovakia in an address to the United States Congress declared that the salvation of the world lies not in slick political slogans about freedom and democracy but rather in the human heart. I agree with that."

—ASSOCIATED PRESS, MARCH 8, 1990, AND OTHER REPORTS

YOU WERE TAKEN ABACK AT THE OUTPOURING IN EUROPE AFTER THE FALL OF THE BERLIN WALL. WHAT WERE YOUR THOUGHTS?

"This is something new. They have a freedom to talk and preach and have Bible classes. They are beginning to print thousands of Bibles in the Soviet Union, and in many places I understand that Sunday schools are being opened, which have been forbidden through all these years. They've had 70 years in which none of these things happened. . . . I never thought this would happen in my lifetime."

—ASSOCIATED PRESS, JANUARY 26, 1990

CAN RELIGION GROW UNDER ANY REGIME NO MATTER HOW
REPRESSIVE?
"Christianity has always grown under rulers who didn't believe in
Christ or in God. Yes, the [Soviet] government is atheistic. But I
believe that in this government there are true believers." *(Speaking
about the Soviet Union as an officially atheistic country)*

—ASSOCIATED PRESS, JUNE 17, 1988

WHAT IS THE IMPORTANCE OF THE MIDDLE EAST TO WORLD
PEACE?
"I was studying maps of the Persian Gulf this morning. Many theologians think that is where the Garden of Eden was located. We
know that Abraham came from Ur which is just north of the Persian
Gulf. So much of biblical history is in that area and we must pray for
peace there because it could draw other nations in."

—PR NEWSWIRE, AUGUST 18, 1987

WERE YOU SURPRISED BY THE PEOPLE YOU MET IN THE SOVIET
UNION?
"I found that those people are like us. I'm talking about the people,
not the government. They are people with the same fears, the same
desires, the same anxieties and joys and all the rest.

—UNITED PRESS INTERNATIONAL, MAY 2, 1986

WHEN THE UNITED STATES AND SOVIET UNION WERE IN THE
BEGINNING OF THE EASING OF TENSIONS KNOWN AS
GLASNOST, YOU HAD SOME SUGGESTIONS FOR THE
SUPERPOWER LEADERS. WHAT DID YOU RECOMMEND PUBLICLY
TO BOTH OF THEM?
"There's nothing like personal contact and personal friendship for
getting over obstacles. Both men have appeal. They both smile a lot.

[President Ronald] Reagan is one of the great story-tellers, and [Prime Minister Mikhail] Gorbachev is, too."

—ASSOCIATED PRESS, OCTOBER 11, 1985

IN GOING TO THE SOVIET UNION DURING THE COLD WAR YEARS, WAS THERE A RISK THAT THE USSR WAS JUST USING YOU TO HELP BOLSTER THEIR POSITION IN DISARMAMENT TALKS?

(Asked of Graham after a twelve-day crusade to the Soviet Union)
"Yes, but the risk was worth it for the cause of peace and for the cause of the gospel I preach."

—*CHRISTIAN SCIENCE MONITOR* (BOSTON, MA), SEPTEMBER 27, 1984

WHEN YOU VISITED THE FORMER SOVIET UNION, DID YOU GET THE IMPRESSION THAT THE PEOPLE THERE WANTED PEACE?

"I think that the American and Soviet peoples do not want war. I was told this by people during my trip to your country, and I realized that they were sincere. This is not hard to understand, since we have lived through a terrible war which 40 years ago took away 20,000,000 human lives. We in America have not known a war on our territory in over 100 years. What is needed now are concrete actions and steps by our countries to maintain peace. These steps should be taken as quickly as possible."

—BBC SUMMARY OF WORLD BROADCASTS, SEPTEMBER 26, 1984

BEFORE YOU WENT TO THE SOVIET UNION, THERE WERE MANY MISCONCEPTIONS ABOUT RELIGIOUS LIFE THERE. WHAT WAS YOUR IMPRESSION AFTER YOUR VISIT?

"Many churches are open and active, and it is my understanding that they normally are allowed to carry out their work on church premises as long as they abide by the Government's requirements. At the same time, the Soviet Union does not allow churches to be a rallying point for what it considers anti-Soviet activities."

— *THE NEW YORK TIMES*, SEPTEMBER 22, 1984

WERE THERE ANY RESTRICTIONS PLACED ON YOUR PREACHING AT ORTHODOX AND BAPTIST CHURCHES IN MOSCOW, LENINGRAD, TALLINN, AND NOVOSIBIRSK IN THE FORMER SOVIET UNION?
"The only limitation I have had is that . . . all services have been held only on church property."

—UNITED PRESS INTERNATIONAL, SEPTEMBER 22, 1984

DID YOU GET THE IMPRESSION THAT THE FORMER SOVIET UNION WAS ATHEISTIC?
"I don't think that you could say that the State is atheistic. I think one, to be technical if I might be, the Party is atheistic and the State has the Constitution which regulates the church life in the Soviet Union, and in that Constitution it gives a measure of freedom to worship God within the churches in their own way that they want to worship. I've heard and read that if you have 20 people and a pastor, you can register and become a church, and it is recognized by the government. People have the right to believe or not to believe. I mean you can choose to be an atheist or an agnostic if you want to be, or you can be Christian or you can be Buddhist or Islam or whatever, and I would think that that's true in many countries of the world, both socialist and non-socialist."

—BBC SUMMARY OF WORLD BROADCASTS, SEPTEMBER 21, 1984

WHAT MISCONCEPTIONS DID SOVIET CITIZENS HAVE ABOUT
RELIGION IN THE UNITED STATES?
"They think it is Christian. It is not. It is a secularist, materialistic
country. There are many Christians in America but they are not the
dominant force. The Christian faith should not be judged because of
what America does politically or in any other way." *(Statement made
while addressing two hundred pastors from all over the Soviet Union, at
a Russian Baptist church in Moscow.)*

—UNITED PRESS INTERNATIONAL, SEPTEMBER 21, 1984

HOW DO YOU REMAIN POLITICALLY NEUTRAL WHEN YOU
PREACH IN A COUNTRY THAT MAY HAVE LESS FREEDOM THAN
IN THE UNITED STATES?
"In a host country like this [speaking about the Soviet Union] it's
been my practice through the years never to take political sides and
get involved in their local problems because then it means my own
ministry is limited."

—ASSOCIATED PRESS, MAY 12, 1982

IN WHAT WAY WAS YOUR VISIT TO THE SOVIET UNION A
LOGICAL EXTENSION OF EXISTING RELATIONS BETWEEN THE
TWO COUNTRIES?
"We trade with each other, we have cultural exchanges, and we have
continued political negotiations in spite of our differences. I think it
is now time we move into the spiritual dimension as well."

—*THE WASHINGTON POST,* MARCH 24, 1982

On CRUSADES AND MISSIONS

DO YOU KNOW HOW MANY PEOPLE YOU HAVE REACHED
DURING YOUR CRUSADES?

"My hope is that individuals will be touched by Christ, families will
be touched, I don't know how many. I don't go by numbers. A lot of
people go by numbers. I don't. In some crusades there are immediate
results. In others, it might take 25 years to see the results."

— *THE TENNESSEAN*, MAY 26, 2000

ARE YOU DISAPPOINTED WHEN THE AUDIENCE IS SMALLER
THAN EXPECTED?

"I'm surprised when anyone shows up. I've preached to as many
empty seats as full ones. Whether it's filled or not, people respond."

— *ST. LOUIS POST-DISPATCH* (MISSOURI), OCTOBER 13, 1999

DO YOU SOMETIMES DOUBT THAT YOUR CRUSADES ARE
HELPING PEOPLE?

"I don't know whether we've accomplished much or not. You read the
headlines. . . . Crimes are higher. War is more intense. It seems every
time we settle one problem, another one breaks out. . . . It's one thing
to fill an arena with people. It's another thing to change their hearts."

— *JOURNAL & COURIER* (LAFAYETTE, IN), JUNE 3, 1999

YOUR CRUSADES CAN BRING IN HUNDREDS OF THOUSANDS OF
PEOPLE IN ONE PLACE, BUT IT WAS VERY DIFFERENT IN THE
EARLY DAYS. WHAT WAS THAT LIKE?

"I used to preach on street corners because no church would have
me. . . . I had tremendous experience on the street corners."

— *THE TAMPA TRIBUNE* (FLORIDA), OCTOBER 21, 1998, ON GRAHAM'S RETURN TO TAMPA,

THE CITY WHERE HE HAD PREACHED IN THE STREET, OFTEN IN FRONT OF SALOONS

WHY DO SO MANY HUNDREDS OF THOUSANDS FLOCK TO HEAR
YOU WHEREVER YOU GO?

"Well, part of the answer, I suppose, is that I've been preaching so
long . . . and curiosity . . . but I prefer to think that it's God."

— *LOS ANGELES TIMES,* JULY 7, 1985

CAN ANYBODY PREDICT YOUR LAST MISSION?

"When we were in Dallas, I read in the paper that was probably our
last mission. When we were in San Diego, I read it in the paper, it
may be our last mission. Now in Oklahoma City, I read in the paper
that this might be our last mission. I never say never, because in
God's work, I'm under His direction."

— *DAILY OKLAHOMAN* (OKLAHOMA CITY), JUNE 14, 2003

AFTER YOUR CRUSADE IN NEW YORK CITY IN JUNE 2005,
THE BILLY GRAHAM EVANGELISTIC ASSOCIATION GAVE
OFFICIAL NOTICE THAT IT WAS YOUR LAST CRUSADE. HOW DID
YOU FEEL ABOUT THAT?

"Ruth and I have enjoyed our time together these last few months,
and we both feel at peace about the decision to have the New York
meetings be our last. We know that God can still use us to reach
people with the Gospel message in other ways, and we look forward
to seeing how he will do so."

— CANADIAN PRESS NEWSWIRE, NOVEMBER 15, 2005

WERE YOU CERTAIN THAT NEW YORK WOULD BE YOUR LAST
CRUSADE?

"We hope to come back again someday. I was asked in an interview
if this was our last crusade. I said, 'It probably is—in New York.' But
I also said, 'I never say never.' Never is a bad word, because we never
know."

— *THE NEW YORK TIMES*, JUNE 27, 2005

ARE YOUR CRUSADES WORTH THE EFFORT IF THEY ONLY
CHANGE A FEW PEOPLE?

"One person coming to God for eternal life is worth more than the
whole world. Who knows who that person may be in the future?
That is the mystery of the gospel. You reach one person and you may
reach a whole family or a neighborhood. . . . Some of the seeds [you
sow] falls on bare ground. But some falls on good soil and will return
30-fold, 60-fold or even 100-fold."

— UNITED PRESS INTERNATIONAL, SEPTEMBER 18, 1984

On DEATH

WHAT ADVICE OR WORDS CAN YOU OFFER FOR THOSE
NEARING DEATH?

"Death comes on all, comes for everyone. I'm almost 84, I know that
death is going to come to me in the near future. But because of what
Jesus did on the cross, I'm ready and happy to go. And you can be, too."

— *ASHEVILLE CITIZEN-TIMES*, OCTOBER 19, 2002

HOW WILL GOD SHOW US OUR LIVES WHEN WE DIE?

"Someday there will be a giant screen, and everything you ever did
from the time you were born until the time you died will be on it—and
not just what you did but everything you intended. If you don't remember anything else I say tonight, never forget that God loves you."

— *SAN ANTONIO EXPRESS-NEWS* (TEXAS), OCTOBER 19, 2002

WHAT DID YOU THINK ABOUT WHEN YOU WERE GOING IN AND
OUT OF HOSPITALS, YOUR HEALTH DETERIORATING, AND YOU
THOUGHT YOU MIGHT DIE SOON?

"I've had a great deal of illness in the past two years. . . . I haven't been
able to live a normal life. . . . It's been a difficult time. I thought I was
dying. . . . My whole life came before me. I didn't say to the Lord, 'I'm
a preacher.' I said, 'Oh Lord, I'm a sinner. I still need the cross.'"

— *THE TALLAHASSEE DEMOCRAT*, JUNE 29, 2002

"I've been asked many times, Do I fear death? No, I look forward to death with great anticipation. . . . I'm looking forward to seeing God. I'm looking forward to seeing God face to face, and that could happen any day."

—NEWHOUSE NEWS SERVICE, JUNE 22, 2005

WHAT HAPPENED WHEN YOU THOUGHT YOU WERE DYING?

"That night, I thought I was dying. Or at least I thought I was. I prayed to the Lord, and all of my sins came in front of me that I had done, even as a child. I experienced the greatest peace that I've ever had—and I've never lost it to this day. I'm looking forward to seeing God face to face. And that can happen any day." *(After undergoing brain surgery at the Mayo Clinic in Rochester, Minnesota)*

—*NEWSDAY*, JUNE 22, 2005

DO YOU HAVE YOUR BURIAL PLACE CHOSEN?

"Yes, I've got the place picked out. We're going to be buried—my wife and me will be buried at a place we built, a conference center in North Carolina, where thousands of people come in the summertime to sing, to worship, and it's all marked out. In fact, my colleague, Cliff Barrows, who leads our music and so forth, his wife died. She's buried there."

—CNN'S *LARRY KING LIVE*, MAY 29, 2005

ARE YOU AFRAID OF THE DYING PROCESS?

"I'm not looking forward to the process of dying. I don't like that. I call on people who are dying in my ministry, and I see some of the terrible things that happen to people that are dying. I don't want that, but I will take it if that's the way God wants me to die, because I think that even in that suffering of death, the process of dying, God teaches you many lessons, even in those last hours, those last months of life. And I don't want to miss any of it."

— CNN's *LARRY KING LIVE*, OCTOBER 26, 1998

WOULD YOU LIKE TO PREACH YOUR OWN EULOGY?
"I might preach it myself and put it on a tape and let the people see me preach my own funeral. Then I'd tell some things they never knew before."

— *THE CHARLOTTE OBSERVER* (NORTH CAROLINA), FEBRUARY 11, 1995

IS DEATH THE GREAT EQUALIZER?
"There is a democracy about death. It comes equally to us all and makes us all equal when it comes."

— *THE AMERICAN SPECTATOR*, JUNE 1994, UPON THE DEATH
OF PRESIDENT RICHARD NIXON

On EVANGELISM

WHAT'S YOUR DEFINITION OF EVANGELISM?

"Evangelism is when the Gospel, which is good news, is preached or presented to all people."

— *USA TODAY*, MAY 16, 2005

HOW HAVE EVANGELICAL SCHOLARS CHANGED OVER THE YEARS?

"Christianity has not generally penetrated the intellectual opinion-makers of the world, but we're waking up to this and evangelicals have attained the intellectual level to deal with it. . . . There's a whole crop of new young theologians. Evangelical scholarship can now stand toe to toe with liberal and secular scholars."

—ASSOCIATED PRESS, DECEMBER 31, 1982

WHY DOES EVANGELISM RANK HIGH IN YOUR PRIORITIES?

"Why is evangelism our priority? It isn't simply so our institutions will survive from one generation to the next. It is because of the lost-ness and hopelessness all around us. . . . We are also called to worship and to prayer, and we are called to compassionate service in our world. We should be involved in many other social, educational and family ministries. However, in priority, evangelism comes first."

—*ASIA PULSE*, JULY 31, 2000

WHAT ROLE DOES TELEVISION, RADIO, AND THE INTERNET
PLAY IN THE EVANGELICAL MOVEMENT?

"Thanks to technology, for the first time in human history it truly is possible for us to reach the whole world for Christ." *(Via satellite before an evangelical meeting in Amsterdam)*

—ASSOCIATED PRESS, JULY 30, 2000

WHAT ABOUT THE ABILITY OF MOVIES TO PREACH THE
GOSPEL?

"Early in my ministry, I recognized the fact that not everyone would respond to the Gospel as the result of personal contact through the crusades. Therefore, in the early 1950s, World Wide Pictures was formed and has since produced over 125 films." *(World Wide Pictures was incorporated in 1952 as the motion picture ministry of the Billy Graham Evangelistic Association.)*

—*LOS ANGELES SENTINEL,* MAY 16, 2000

WHAT IS THE ROLE OF THE EVANGELIST?

"The calling of evangelist is one of the great gifts that God has given to the church, and is as important as the seminary professor or church pastor. In the Bible, the evangelist is called ambassador, proclaimer, advocate, and announcer of Good News. He presents this News on a world network when he lifts up Jesus Christ. A great need in the church today is to recognize and dignify the gift of the evangelist."

—*PRINCE GEORGE CITIZEN* (BRITISH COLUMBIA), MAY 13, 2000

HOW CAN WE GET BACK TO THE BASICS OF THE EVANGELICAL
MOVEMENT?

"We must go back and search the Word of God to discover what we need to do for the extension of the Kingdom in our day. That is the reason we have convened this conference." *(Via satellite before an evangelical meeting in Amsterdam)*

—CANADA NEWSWIRE, JULY 30, 2000

TO WHAT DID YOU ATTRIBUTE THE DECLINE OF CHURCHES IN EUROPE?
"One of the reasons churches are dying in Europe is because they have departed from the Scriptures. Here [in the U.S.], the group that is growing the fastest is the evangelicals, who hold to a strong belief in the Bible."

—*OTTAWA CITIZEN*, MAY 31, 1998

WHAT IS THE CHALLENGE OF EVANGELICAL MINISTERS?
(A question posed upon Graham's announcement of Amsterdam 2000, the first worldwide evangelism conference in fourteen years)
"Decay in the societies of the world, consternation in the governments, and a deep heart-cry for revival throughout the Church of our Lord Jesus Christ all point to the need of the world for our Savior. . . . The Lord of the harvest has many servants who are doing extraordinary work in bringing the Gospel to those who still sit in darkness. Their stories need to be known, their strategies multiplied, their commitments deepened and their fellowship enriched within the Body of Christ."

—CANADA NEWSWIRE, SEPTEMBER 15, 1998

YOU WERE HAPPY TO SEE SO MANY OTHER CLERGY AT YOUR CRUSADES. DID THAT RAISE YOUR SPIRITS?
"A number of clergy have said this is the first time many pastors have gotten to know each other. Wouldn't it be great if we could forget our denominations and just be people of God." *(Speaking about the Bay Area Crusade in Oakland)*

—PR NEWSWIRE, OCTOBER 27, 1997

WHAT DO ALL EVANGELISTS HAVE IN COMMON?
"When you're an evangelist, you just preach one message—the good news of the gospel. So many people have hurts and know they have sins in their lives. I want to bring a new joy in their lives and the assurance they can go to heaven."

—*ST. PAUL PIONEER PRESS* (MINNESOTA), JUNE 18, 1996

WHAT IS THE ROLE OF SPOUSES TO EVANGELISTS?
"The spouse is extremely important in the work of the evangelist. I don't think an evangelist can do his work properly if he doesn't have his spouse with him and backing him and knows that he has the love of his wife and his children."

—NEWS CONFERENCE PRIOR TO THE NORTH AMERICAN CONFERENCE
FOR ITINERANT EVANGELISTS (NACIE 94) AT THE COMMONWEALTH
CONVENTION CENTER IN LOUISVILLE, KENTUCKY, PR NEWSWIRE, JUNE 29, 1994

DO YOU REJECT THE NOTION THAT ONLY PROFESSIONAL
PREACHERS SHOULD PREACH THE GOSPEL?
"When the Lord said to go and preach the Gospel to all the people, I don't think he was just talking to paid professionals. He was talking to the whole church."

—ASSOCIATED PRESS, MAY 28, 1993

WHAT DO YOU SAY TO PEOPLE WHO CONTEND THAT THE
CHURCH'S ROLE SHOULD BE MORE ABOUT SOCIAL AND MORAL
REFORM?
"There are people today in the church and out of the church that say that we ought to spend all of our time in moral and social reform. You could have moral reform and social reform, but it's not going to accomplish utopia and the kingdom of heaven until the hearts of people have been changed. And I'm convinced that we have a moral

responsibility; we have a social responsibility. I'm convinced the gospel has something to say to every social issue. But I'm also convinced that the main task of evangelism is to win souls to Jesus Christ."

—FROM AUDIO FILE TAPE, NPR'S *WEEKEND EDITION*, FEBRUARY 16, 1992

HOW HAVE YOU BROADENED YOUR THOUGHTS IN TERMS OF OTHER PEOPLE'S BELIEFS WITHIN THE CHRISTIAN COMMUNITY?
"In relation to others, I used to think that if a person hadn't experienced what I had experienced, he wasn't a believer. It was my own ignorance. I had not had the opportunity to fellowship with people in other communities before."

—*CALGARY HERALD* (ALBERTA, CANADA), DECEMBER 7, 1991

HOW MUCH DAMAGE TO THE CREDIBILITY OF THE EVANGELICAL MOVEMENT DID PREACHERS LIKE JIMMY SWAGGART AND JIM BAKKER DO?
"They caused no harm because they are not evangelists. The newspapers say they are evangelists. But an evangelist is a person who communicates. He communicates the gospel, which means good news. God loves you. . . . You communicate by how you live."

—*NEWSDAY*, SEPTEMBER 19, 1991

ARE THERE DIFFERENT METHODS OF EVANGELISM?
"I think all denominations need to get involved in evangelism. I think that the whole church realizes something has to be done. We have lost a great many of our moral values, they need to be restored. One of the great ways they can be restored—the only way—is through a spiritual awakening and revival. From the Christian point of view, that comes from the proclamation of the Gospel of Christ. . . . There are many methods of evangelism. The best is person-to-person, church evangelism. We are hoping this crusade

will stir up churches to go out and do the same thing, perhaps using different methods."

—PR NEWSWIRE, JULY 16, 1990

WHAT WAS THE EFFECT TO THE EVANGELICAL MOVEMENT WHEN JIM BAKKER WAS CONVICTED OF FRAUD, WITH PROSECUTORS CHARGING THAT HE DIVERTED MORE THAN $3 MILLION OF MINISTRY MONEY TO PAY FOR HIS LAVISH LIFESTYLE?

"This verdict doesn't bother the work of the Lord; the work of the church continues to go on no matter what happens. God's work is not dependent upon one person—it is dependent upon the Holy Spirit. There are still countless thousands of men and women in the ministry—serving as pastors, teachers, missionaries and evangelists— being faithful to what God has called them to do, many of them on very low incomes."

—ASSOCIATED PRESS, OCTOBER 6, 1989

"The work of the Lord continues. One bad meal at a restaurant doesn't mean you quit eating. No, I'm not worried about the future of the church. God is sovereign. His will is going to be worked out. I think this is a great time in the history of the church. Its opportunities have never been greater."

—ASSOCIATED PRESS, DECEMBER 18, 1987

"Sometimes I fear that our message is in danger of being diluted. Somewhere along the line we have lost the authority and the cutting edge of our message. . . . The world looks at us [evangelists] and they see the same way of living, the same motives, the same petty jealousies that characterize the world, or they see where leaders have yielded to the temptations of money, lust or power, and they see little reason to believe our message can really change their lives. That is why there must be renewal within before there can be witness without to a restless and depraved world."

— *LOS ANGELES TIMES*, JUNE 20, 1987

HAS PLEADING FOR MONEY HURT THE EVANGELICAL MOVEMENT?

"I have seen certain evangelists who have made chills go up and down my spine. I felt they were going too far in appeals for money. . . . Pleading for money is damaging to the entire evangelical movement. . . . Too much emotion and too much criticism of the church also cheapens the work of evangelists."

— *LOS ANGELES TIMES*, MAY 16, 1985

WHAT HAVE YOU TRIED TO DO TO RAISE THE PUBLIC PERCEPTION OF EVANGELISTS?

"I've tried to lift the standard of the evangelist. Sometimes the standards drop below what I think are biblical standards. . . . In the political arena, I think there were pastors and evangelists who went too far, from my point of view, both from the left and from the right."

— *THE NEW YORK TIMES*, JANUARY 3, 1985,

IN DISCUSSING HIS BOOK *STANDARDS FOR THE EVANGELIST*

WHEN TV EVANGELISTS EMPHASIZE MONEY INSTEAD OF PREACHING THE GOSPEL, DO THEY MISS THE MAIN MESSAGE?

"As Christian evangelists . . . we should speak out on moral issues, but we should not use our programs to endorse political candidates or causes. There is a danger when TV preachers begin to beg too frequently and too fervently. Money is a means: It must never be the message."

— *TV GUIDE*, MARCH 5, 1983

DO YOU SEE ANY PARALLELS BETWEEN YOU AND THE POPE AS
FAR AS SPREADING GOD'S WORD IS CONCERNED?

"When I hear the Pope plead, 'Come to Christ, come to Christ,' he
sounds like me when I invite people at the end of my services to come
forward and make a decision for Christ."

—*NEWSWEEK*, APRIL 26, 1982

WHAT IS MANKIND'S GREATEST ACT OF LOVE TOWARD EACH
OTHER?

"I am convinced the greatest act of love we can ever perform for
another person is to tell them about God's love for them in Christ.
Some of the greatest social movements in history have been the fruit
of true evangelical revivals."

—UNITED PRESS INTERNATIONAL, JULY 30, 1981

WHAT ARE THE DANGERS OF TELEVANGELISTS WHO
CONTINUALLY PUMMEL THEIR VIEWERS WITH REQUESTS FOR
MONEY?

"Instead of trusting God to supply our financial needs, we may rely
on a sophisticated direct-mail campaign, give-aways or an advertising agency with a proven track record. We should trust God."

—ASSOCIATED PRESS, JANUARY 28, 1981

IN YOUR OPINION, WHAT'S THE MAIN GOAL OF BEING AN
EVANGELIST?

"I think that the Gospel is the main thing. If you get off from preaching the Gospel, you get involved in so many things that divide
people, and I'm trying to unite people in hearing the Gospel and
receiving Christ as their savior . . . but being an evangelist I feel my
job is to just preach the Gospel."

—*THE DAILY NEWS OF LOS ANGELES*, NOVEMBER 17, 2004

DID YOU SEE POPE JOHN PAUL II AS AN EVANGELIST OF SORTS?

"In his own way, he saw himself as an evangelist. He was convinced that the complex problems of our world are ultimately moral and spiritual in nature, and only Christ can set us free from the shackles of sin and greed and violence."

— *WINSTON-SALEM JOURNAL* (NORTH CAROLINA), APRIL 3, 2005

DO YOU TAKE OFFENSE AT HOW SOME OTHER SO-CALLED EVANGELISTS PREACH THE GOSPEL, PERHAPS DOING IT JUST FOR THE MONEY?

"I'm not interested in what impact I have. I'm interested in the whole gospel of Christ. Whoever preaches it. Paul, the Apostle Paul, says, 'However the gospel is preached I rejoice.' It may be that some are preaching for money and some for personal gain, but he said whoever preaches it I rejoice. And I do."

— *NEWSDAY,* SEPTEMBER 17, 1990

WHAT DO YOU THINK ABOUT THE MIXING OF RELIGION AND POLITICS?

"I would hate to see either right-wing or left-wing groups using evangelical Christians for political ends. In the long term, it will dilute the Gospel that we preach."

— *THE WASHINGTON POST,* DECEMBER 7, 1980

PARTIAL LIST OF
AWARDS AND HONORS

"Ten Most Admired Men in the World," from the Gallup Poll since 1955, a total of forty-eight times, including forty-one consecutive—more than any other individual in the world, placing him at the head of the overall list of those most admired by Americans for the past four decades

Clergyman of the Year from the National Pilgrim Society

Distinguished Service Medal of the Salvation Army

Who's Who in America annually since 1954

Freedoms Foundation Distinguished Persons Award (numerous years)

Gold Medal Award, National Institute of Social Science, New York, 1957

Annual Gutenberg Award of the Chicago Bible Society, 1962

Gold Award of the George Washington Carver Memorial Institute, 1964, for contribution to race relations, presented by Senator Javits (NY)

Speaker of the Year Award, 1964

Golden Plate Award, American Academy of Achievement, 1965

Horatio Alger Award, 1965

National Citizenship Award by the Military Chaplains Association of the U.S.A., 1965

Wisdom Award of Honor, 1965

Big Brother of the Year Award, at the White House, Washington, DC, 1966, for contribution to the welfare of children

The Torch of Liberty Plaque by the Anti-Defamation League of B'nai B'rith, 1969

George Washington Honor Medal from Freedoms Foundation of Valley Forge, Pennsylvania, for his sermon "The Violent Society," 1969

Honored by Morality in Media for "fostering the principles of truth, taste, inspiration and love in media," 1969

International Brotherhood Award from the National Conference of Christians and Jews, 1971

Distinguished Service Award from the National Association of Broadcasters, 1972

Franciscan International Award, 1972

Sylvanus Thayer Award from United States Military Academy Association of Graduates at West Point (the most prestigious award the United States Military Academy gives to a U.S. citizen), 1972

George Washington Medal Award for Patriotism from Freedoms Foundation of Valley Forge, 1974

Direct Selling Association's Salesman of the Decade award, 1975

Philip Award from the Association of United Methodist Evangelists, 1976

First National Interreligious Award, American Jewish Committee, 1977

Distinguished Communications Medal, Southern Baptist Radio and Television Commission, 1977

Jabotinsky Centennial Medal presented by The Jabotinsky Foundation, 1980

Religious Broadcasting Hall of Fame award, 1981

Templeton Foundation Prize for Progress in Religion award, 1982

Presidential Medal of Freedom, the nation's highest civilian award, 1983

National Religious Broadcasters Award of Merit, 1986

North Carolina Award in Public Service, 1986

Congressional Gold Medal, the highest honor Congress can bestow on a private citizen, 1996

Good Housekeeping Most Admired Men Poll, 1997, number one for five years in a row and sixteenth time in top 10

Inducted into the Gospel Music Hall of Fame by the Gospel Music Association—the first non-musician to be inducted, 1999

Ronald Reagan Presidential Foundation Freedom Award, for monumental and lasting contributions to the cause of freedom, 2000

Honorary Knight Commander of the order of the British Empire (KBE) for his international contribution to civic and religious life over sixty years, 2001

SOURCE: BILLY GRAHAM EVANGELISTIC ASSOCIATION

On FAITH

"We must trust God when the way is dark and seems unbearable,
and look forward to seeing them in heaven." *(In a note written to relatives and friends of the Odum family, six of whom were killed in a traffic accident)*

— *THE STATE* (COLUMBIA, SC), JULY 30, 2000

"I am disappointed at this turn of events [ill health]. But I have great
peace that this is God's plan for me." *(Response with regard to not being
healthy enough to attend an evangelical conference)*

— *SUNDAY EXPRESS*, JULY 30, 2000

"The wounds of this tragedy are deep, but the courage and the faith
and determination of the people of Oklahoma City are even deeper.
Let the healing begin."

— *PALM BEACH POST* (FLORIDA), OCTOBER 23, 1998

HAVE YOU HAD DOUBTS ABOUT YOUR FAITH?

"I've had doubts about myself—about my own experience of living in Christ, helping people, doing the things Jesus taught us to do, taking up the cross and following him. I've had doubts about myself, not about God."

— *SAN ANTONIO EXPRESS-NEWS* (TEXAS), APRIL 3, 1997

HOW DO YOU COMFORT PARENTS WHO HAVE LOST A CHILD?

"I just tell them that God loves them, that there's a reason for it, and just accept the fact that God is a God of love, and he's not going to let anything happen to you or to that child unless there was a reason for it.... And many of those children that we read about and hear about, if they have not reached the age of accountability, the Bible teaches, they're going to go straight to Heaven, no matter what happened."

— CNN's *LARRY KING LIVE*, JANUARY 21, 1997

•

WHAT DID YOU TELL MOURNERS AFTER THE MURRAH FEDERAL BUILDING BOMBING ABOUT HOW THIS AND OTHER TRAGEDIES COULD AFFECT THEM?

"Times like this will do one of two things. It will either make us hard and bitter and angry at God or make us tender and open and teach us to reach out and trust in faith.... I pray you will not let bitterness and poison creep into your soul."

— *ST. PETERSBURG TIMES* (FLORIDA), APRIL 24, 1995

HOW CAN YOU COMFORT PEOPLE AFTER NATURAL DISASTERS LIKE EARTHQUAKES?

"We do not know why these tragedies happen. But we know that He can use what has happened as a result of this disaster to bring people closer to Him and closer to one another."

— *LOS ANGELES TIMES*, JANUARY 24, 1994, IN A STATEMENT FOLLOWING AN EARTHQUAKE IN CALIFORNIA

HOW DO YOU HANDLE GROWING SKEPTICISM ABOUT
CHRISTIANITY AND CRITICISM THAT THE BIBLE IS NOT THE
WORD OF GOD BUT SIMPLY STORIES WRITTEN BY PEOPLE?
"I have found that if I say, 'The Bible says' and 'God says,' I get
results. I have decided I am not going to wrestle with these questions
any longer."

—THE SAN DIEGO UNION-TRIBUNE, MAY 11, 2003

On Friends and Acquaintances

You had great respect for Cardinal John O'Connor, head of the New York Archdiocese. What were your thoughts when he died in 2000 at age eighty?

"The church has lost a great warrior, and the country has lost a great patriot, who will long be remembered. He was a bold and courageous man, who stood firmly for what he believed."

— *Seattle Post-Intelligencer*, May 4, 2000

"What are your thoughts about Nation of Islam leader Louis Farrakhan?

"His views and my views will be very far apart, and it would be very difficult for us [to meet]. We could be friends, but it would be very difficult for us to say that we are the same, or that we could be the same religiously."

— *The Commercial Appeal* (Memphis, TN), January 3, 2000

Who would you choose as one of the greatest people of the twentieth century?

"Pope John Paul II. I admire his courage, determination, intellectual abilities and his understanding of Catholic, Protestant and Orthodox differences, and the attempt at some form of reconciliation."

—*THE VIRGINIAN-PILOT* (NORFOLK), JANUARY 1, 2000

YOU'VE SAID THAT YOU REGRET NOT HAVING JOHN F. KENNEDY JR. AT YOUR HOUSE IN NORTH CAROLINA FOR AN EXTENDED MEETING. CONFLICTING SCHEDULES CAUSED THE DELAY, AND HE DIED A SHORT TIME LATER IN AN AIRPLANE CRASH. WHAT WERE THE CIRCUMSTANCES, AND WHAT OTHER THOUGHTS DO YOU HAVE ABOUT HIM?

"He said, 'I really want to talk to you.' We never got to do it, and that's been one of the greatest regrets of my life, because I loved that young man."

—*ARKANSAS DEMOCRAT-GAZETTE* (LITTLE ROCK), OCTOBER 2, 1999

"He was headed towards doing something great. Because he had all the attributes of greatness that we look for in a leader."

—*SAN ANTONIO EXPRESS-NEWS* (TEXAS), JULY 24, 1999

WHAT WERE YOUR IMPRESSIONS OF THE DALAI LAMA?

"He's a man who has exuded a great deal of love and set an example of love to people."

—*BOSTON HERALD*, SEPTEMBER 28, 1999

WHAT SIMPLE ADVICE DID YOU HAVE FOR SINGER JOHNNY CASH, WHO WAS STRUGGLING TO COME BACK FROM A LIFE OF SIN AND EXCESS?

"Be who you are, and do what you do."

—*CHICAGO SUN-TIMES*, NOVEMBER 19, 1997

YOU MET WITH CHINESE PRESIDENT JIANG ZENIM AT HIS
REQUEST ON A VISIT TO THE UNITED STATES. WHAT WERE
YOUR IMPRESSIONS OF HIM?

"I found the President to be very warm and personable. He is highly
intelligent and curious about our country, and has clearly learned much
during his trip here. I told him I felt that he had a very successful trip,
and hoped that he could come again for a more extensive visit."

—PR NEWSWIRE, NOVEMBER 2, 1997

WHAT CAN WE LEARN FROM THE LIVES OF PRINCESS DIANA
AND MOTHER TERESA?

"Princess Diana's death reminds us of the brevity of life, while Mother
Teresa reminds us of the meaning of life."

—OAKLAND POST, SEPTEMBER 28, 1997

WHAT WERE YOUR THOUGHTS ABOUT MOTHER TERESA UPON
HER PASSING?

"It was my privilege to be with her on several occasions. The first
time was at the Home of Dying Destitutes in Calcutta. I had a wonderful hour of fellowship in the Lord with her just at sunset, and I
will never forget the sounds, the smells and the strange beauty of that
place. When she walked into the room to greet me, I felt that I was,
indeed, meeting a saint."

—THE NEW YORK BEACON, SEPTEMBER 17, 1997

WHAT WERE YOUR THOUGHTS ABOUT PRINCESS DIANA UPON
HER PASSING?

"Princess Diana was an international hero who has provided a win-
dow into the human heart."

—SUNDAY MAIL (SCOTLAND), SEPTEMBER 7, 1997

WHAT CAN WE LEARN FROM THE PREACHING OF DR. MARTIN LUTHER KING JR.?

"'I think some of the speeches that the Rev. Martin Luther King made a generation ago should be restudied for their application today. Only repentance and faith in God will lead to the nonviolence that Martin Luther King preached. Only God can change the human heart."

— *PITTSBURGH POST-GAZETTE*, JUNE 19, 1996

WHAT WERE YOUR THOUGHTS ABOUT ISRAEL'S PRIME MINISTER, YITZAK RABIN, UPON HIS ASSASSINATION?

"Sometimes only a man who has seen the horrors of war can fully appreciate the urgency of peace, and I believe that was the case with Prime Minister Rabin."

— ASSOCIATED PRESS, NOVEMBER 4, 1995

WHAT WAS YOUR OPINION OF SAM WALTON, FOUNDER OF WAL-MART?

"The simplicity of lifestyle, the deep religious commitment and the overwhelming success in business, all made him a role model for all Americans."

— *STAR TRIBUNE* (MINNEAPOLIS, MN), SEPTEMBER 13, 1992, CITING A BLURB ON THE BACK OF SAM WALTON'S AUTOBIOGRAPHY, *MADE IN AMERICA: MY STORY*

WHAT'S YOUR OPINION OF SADDAM HUSSEIN?

"Saddam Hussein is a remarkable incarnation of what could be one of the greatest Satanic powers."

— *NEWSDAY* (NEW YORK), SEPTEMBER 24, 1990

YET, YOU DON'T AGREE WITH OTHERS THAT HUSSEIN IS THE ANTICHRIST?

"I've heard this talk that Saddam Hussein could be the Antichrist, but I cannot agree with that. . . . Historians tell us that people thought Napoleon was the Antichrist, they thought Mussolini was the Antichrist and they thought Hitler was the Antichrist."

— UNITED PRESS INTERNATIONAL, SEPTEMBER 11, 1990

WHAT WAS IT LIKE TO MEET ITINERANT PREACHERS WHO MAINLY MINISTER TO UNDERDEVELOPED COUNTRIES?

(Question posed at an international conference of eight thousand Christian mission workers, most of them from the third world, in Amsterdam's convention center)

"Most have never been in an airplane or Western city before. Many of them have scars . . . and have been in prison for their faith. These are people on the cutting edge in the far places of the world. They have paid a greater price than I will ever pay. Most of them will be on the front row of heaven compared to me."

— *CHICAGO TRIBUNE*, JULY 14, 1986

WHAT THOUGHTS DID YOU HAVE ABOUT EGYPTIAN PRESIDENT ANWAR SADAT AFTER HIS ASSASSINATION?

"He was truly one of the giants among world leaders. It is both tragic and ironic that this man, who worked so diligently for an end to violence, was himself a victim of violence."

— UNITED PRESS INTERNATIONAL, OCTOBER 6, 1981

WHAT WAS POPE PAUL VI'S LEGACY?

"Pope Paul presided over the Roman Catholic Church when it was going through one of the most critical periods in its history. In one sense, he witnessed a revolution within the Roman Catholic world that has developed for decades. In another sense, he sought to give that revolution direction and guidance."

— *THE WASHINGTON POST*, AUGUST 7, 1978

WHEN YOU MET POPE JOHN PAUL II, WHAT FEELING DID YOU
HAVE?
"I felt as if we had known each other for years." *(Following a thirty-minute meeting with Pope John Paul II)*

— *WORLD* MAGAZINE, OCTOBER 25, 2003

YOU HAVE BEEN VERY GRATEFUL FOR GEORGE BEVERLY SHEA,
WHO HAS SUNG WITH YOU ON YOUR CRUSADES FOR MORE
THAN FIFTY YEARS. HOW IMPORTANT WAS BEV TO YOUR WORK?
"I would feel lost getting up to preach if Bev were not there to prepare the way through an appropriate song. . . . I've been listening to Bev Shea sing for more than 50 years, and I would still rather hear him sing than anyone else I know."

— *OTTAWA CITIZEN*, JULY 19, 2002

"Songs can touch and open a heart to hear God when sermons and preaching may fall on deaf ears. Music is such a universal language, and God has used Bev to be an instrument to touch and enrich lives."

— *THE KANSAS CITY STAR*, APRIL 10, 2004, QUOTING FROM THE FOREWORD
TO SHEA'S BOOK, *HOW SWEET THE SOUND: AMAZING STORIES AND
GRACE-FILLED REFLECTIONS ON BELOVED HYMNS AND GOSPEL SONGS*

HOW WOULD YOU RATE LARRY KING'S INTERVIEW SKILLS?
"When I went in to be interviewed [by you], I was very relaxed. When I came out, I was quite tense. I knew that I had been interviewed by one of the greatest persons to ever interview me because you have such penetrating questions and I have appreciated your friendship all these years."

—CNN's *LARRY KING LIVE*, NOVEMBER 29, 2003, ON TV HOST
AND INTERVIEWER LARRY KING'S SEVENTIETH BIRTHDAY

HOW CLOSE WERE YOU TO SINGER JOHNNY CASH AND HIS
WIFE, JUNE CARTER?

"Johnny Cash was not only a legend, but a close personal friend . . .
a good man who struggled with many challenges . . . a deeply religious man. . . . Ruth and I took a number of vacations with them. . . .
They both were like a brother and sister to Ruth and me. We loved
them. . . . I look forward to seeing Johnny and June in heaven one day."

— *CALGARY HERALD* (ALBERTA, CANADA), OCTOBER 11, 2003

WHAT WERE YOUR WORDS UPON THE DEATH OF POPE JOHN
PAUL II?

"Pope John Paul II was unquestionably the most influential voice for
morality and peace in the world during the last 100 years. His
extraordinary gifts, his strong Catholic faith, and his experience of
human tyranny and suffering in his native Poland all shaped him, and
yet he was respected by men and women from every conceivable
background across the world. He was truly one of those rare individuals whose legacy will endure long after he has gone."

— *THE TIMES-PICAYUNE* (NEW ORLEANS), APRIL 3, 2005

On GROWING OLDER

HOW HAS YOUR PERSPECTIVE CHANGED AS YOU'VE GOTTEN
OLDER?
"The center of my life now is my children [the Grahams have 3
daughters and 2 sons]. We've got 19 grandchildren and 27 great-
grandchildren. I don't know all of them. Some of them are coming
here, I'm told. I wish they all could be here."

—ASHEVILLE CITIZEN-TIMES (NORTH CAROLINA), MARCH 10, 2006

HAS YOUR ATTITUDE MELLOWED ABOUT CHRISTIAN LEADERS
WHO GO ON TELEVISION AND SAY, "YOU ARE CONDEMNED
AND YOU WILL LIVE IN HELL IF YOU DO NOT ACCEPT JESUS
CHRIST"?
"They have a right to say that, and they are true to a certain extent,
but I don't—that's not my calling. My calling is to preach the love
of God and the forgiveness of God and the fact that He does forgive us. That's what the cross is all about, what the resurrection is
all about, that's the gospel. And you can get off on all kinds of different side trends, and in my earlier ministry, I did the same, but as
I got older, I guess I became more mellow and more forgiving and
more loving. And the Jerry Falwells and people like that, I love
them; I thank God for their ministry; he has a great university and
two or three of my grandchildren have gone there, and they have

64

had a tremendous change in their lives for being there, and some of the other people are the same way, but at the other end of the extreme."

— CNN's *LARRY KING LIVE*, JUNE 26, 2005

IS GROWING OLD AND STILL BEING ABLE TO PREACH A
PRIVILEGE?
"I expect I may be one of the oldest evangelists in history that is still holding meetings like this. And it's a great privilege, and I thank God for the privilege, and I intend to preach as long as I live. I don't know how long that'll be, but I really appreciate the privilege of being here."

— *THE DALLAS MORNING NEWS*, JUNE 20, 2001

HAS YOUR AGE DAMPENED YOUR STRENGTH TO PROCLAIM THE
GOSPEL?
"Although my strength is more limited now that I am in my 80s, my burden to proclaim the gospel is as strong as ever."

— *TULSA WORLD* (OKLAHOMA), JUNE 7, 2003

WERE YOU EXCITED WHEN YOU TURNED EIGHTY?
"That's not the one I want to celebrate. I want to celebrate my 100th birthday. . . . I want to hang around so I can help others and steer them and encourage them."

— *THE ATLANTA JOURNAL AND CONSTITUTION*, NOVEMBER 7, 1998

WHAT KIND OF PHYSICAL TOLL DOES PREACHING TAKE ON
YOU, ESPECIALLY WHEN YOU PASSED SEVENTY-FIVE?
"There have been times . . . I've come down from the platform absolutely exhausted. I feel like I've been wrestling with the devil, who has been doing everything in his power to keep those people

from getting a clear message of the Gospel. . . . Some sort of physical energy goes out of me and I feel terribly weak. I'm depleted."

— *TIME* MAGAZINE, NOVEMBER 15, 1993

HOW HAVE YOUR THOUGHTS AND BELIEFS ABOUT LIFE CHANGED AS YOU'VE GOTTEN OLDER?

"How brief life is. The average person lives as though he's going to live forever. . . . When I was young, I used to think I had a million years out ahead of me. But now that I've turned 65, I've begun to rethink that."

—ASSOCIATED PRESS, JANUARY 16, 1984

DID YOU EVER THINK YOU WOULD REACH INTO YOUR EIGHTIES?

"I never dreamed that I would live to be 85. I am grateful to the Lord for the strength he gives me to hold additional crusades."

— *NATIONAL CATHOLIC REPORTER*, NOVEMBER 28, 2003

DID YOU EVER SEE YOURSELF PREACHING SO LONG?

"It's a privilege for me and for me to be able to preach at my age of 86, and I never dreamed that I'd be preaching like this and especially in a stadium, and nobody in history that I've read and that does the work of evangelism has ever gone this long in their lives."

—NBC'S *TODAY*, NOVEMBER 22, 2004, SPEAKING ABOUT HIS CRUSADE AT MADISON SQUARE GARDEN IN NEW YORK CITY

BOOKS WRITTEN BY BILLY GRAHAM

1947: *Calling Youth to Christ*

1952: Author of syndicated newspaper column My Answer,
carried by newspapers across the country, with a combined ·
circulation of five million readers

1953: *I Saw Your Sons at War*

1953: *Peace with God*—over two million copies sold in thirty-
eight languages, revised and expanded in 1984

1955: *Freedom from the Seven Deadly Sins*

1955: *The Secret of Happiness*

1958: *Billy Graham Talks to Teenagers*

1960: *My Answers*

1960: *Billy Graham Answers Your Questions*

1965: *World Aflame* —The *New York Times* and *Time* magazine
best-seller lists for several weeks

1969: *The Challenge*

1971: *The Jesus Generation*

1975: *Angels: God's Secret Agents*—*Publishers Weekly* and *New York
Times* best-seller lists (twenty-one weeks each); Evangelical
Christian Publishers Association (ECPA) Platinum Book
Award

1977: *How to Be Born Again*

1978: *The Holy Spirit*—ECPA Gold Book Award

1981: *Till Armageddon*—ECPA Platinum Book Award

1983: *Approaching Hoofbeats: The Four Horsemen of the
Apocalypse*—The *New York Times* best-seller list; ECPA
Gold Book Award

1984: *A Biblical Standard for Evangelists*
1986: *Unto the Hills*
1987: *Facing Death and the Life After*—Christian Booksellers
   Association best-seller list (twenty-one weeks)
1988: *Answers to Life's Problems*
1991: *Hope for the Troubled Heart*
1992: *Storm Warning*
1997: *Just as I Am*
2002: *Hope for Each Day*

On HEALTH MATTERS

DOCTORS TOLD YOU TO "SLOW DOWN" FROM YOUR BUSY
SCHEDULE FOR ABOUT SIX MONTHS, BECAUSE THEY WERE
CONCERNED ABOUT SEVERAL HEALTH ISSUES. WHAT WAS
YOUR RESPONSE TO THIS REQUEST?

"They said I should have total rest and stay away from preaching, the telephone and even writing. I intend to do the very best I can to obey them. After all, I'm nearing 62 and have been crusading since 1949— longer than any other evangelist. . . . I'll never retire from preaching. I may retire from the organization which bears my name, that I have very little to do with."

—ASSOCIATED PRESS, APRIL 3, 1980, AND *THE WASHINGTON POST*, APRIL 23, 1980

WHY DID YOU STOP TAKING QUESTIONS AT PRESS
CONFERENCES?

"I used to hold press conferences, but I noticed the pope never holds press conferences. So I think I'll do what he does as I get older. As you can see, I'm shaking now. I can't stand for very long at a time."

—*THE SAN DIEGO UNION-TRIBUNE*, MAY 7, 2003

HAS BEING HOSPITALIZED CHANGED YOUR WAY OF THINKING?
"I have experienced several deep spiritual moments during my hospitalization, and feel that God has given me new vision and new strength for extended ministry in the future."

— *THE STATE* (COLUMBIA, SC), JULY 22, 2000

WHAT CONCESSIONS HAVE YOU MADE TO ACCOMMODATE YOUR HEALTH?
"I have to sit most of the time. I can't do receiving lines much because I don't have good balance. But the moment I take that pulpit, I feel like a young man again."

—ASSOCIATED PRESS, MAY 26, 2000

HAS AGEING CHANGED YOUR MESSAGE OR JUST THE DELIVERY?
"The message hasn't changed. I just don't yell as loud or put as much vigor into it as I used to."

— *THE KANSAS CITY STAR* (KANSAS AND MISSOURI), OCTOBER 17, 1999, CITING
COMMENTS AT A CRUSADE IN KANSAS CITY MORE THAN TEN YEARS EARLIER

WHY DOES GOD MAKE US ILL?
"God sends us illness to keep us from depending on ourselves. It makes us put total dependence on God."

— *ST. LOUIS POST-DISPATCH* (MISSOURI), JUNE 2, 1999

WHERE DO YOU GET THE STRENGTH TO PREACH WHEN YOU'RE TIRED OR ILL?
"When I put my hand on the pulpit, I know people are praying, and I feel the strength and power of the Lord."

— *OTTAWA CITIZEN*, MAY 9, 1998

WHEN YOU FIRST SHOWED OUTWARD SIGNS OF PARKINSON'S DISEASE, DID THE AUDIENCE NOTICE?

"I don't think that when I'm preaching anybody can tell. Once in a while I can't think of the next sentence or the next thought. It does affect memory a little, but not much. I'm feeling fine."

—*ALBUQUERQUE JOURNAL* (NEW MEXICO), MAY 3, 1998

IS AIDS A JUDGMENT OF GOD?

"I could not say for sure, but I think so." [Later, Graham retracted this statement.] "I remember saying it, and I immediately regretted it and almost went back and clarified the statement. . . . I don't believe that, and I don't know why I said it. To say God has judged people with AIDS would be very wrong and very cruel. I would like to say that I am very sorry for what I said."

—*ST. LOUIS POST-DISPATCH* (MISSOURI), OCTOBER 11, 1993

WHY DO WE HAVE DISEASES?

"I don't know. We've had many diseases in the past, like polio or other diseases . . . that have wiped out thousands of people throughout the world. Was it judgment from God? I could not say. I know God sent plagues upon Egypt when they refused to let the people of Israel go. I know that God has sent plagues in biblical times. Whether this is a plague from God to warn us, I do not know. But I would say we would better take it as a warning because it is a terrible thing."

—*THE POST-STANDARD* (SYRACUSE, NY), APRIL 28, 1989

YOU'VE SAID THAT TAKING MEDICINES CAN BE AN ACT OF
FAITH IN DOCTORS, JUST LIKE HAVING FAITH IN GOD. CAN
YOU EXPLAIN THIS?

"There is one little tiny pill I take one hour before I have breakfast. I
take that little tiny pill . . . I don't know what's in it. I take it by faith
and belief in the doctor. . . . Within a week of taking it, the trembling
[from Parkinson's disease] went out of my hands. . . . We take things
every day on faith. God has given us a prescription that must be
received, taken and applied."

— DURING THE COLUMBUS CRUSADE SERMON,

THE COLUMBUS DISPATCH (OHIO), SEPTEMBER 24, 1993

HOW SHOULD CHRISTIANS APPROACH THE ISSUE OF AIDS?

"AIDS is a huge problem, something which could eventually destroy
a large part of the human race. I think Christians should go out of
their way to love people who have AIDS. They, more than anyone,
are open and receptive to the Gospel."

— PR NEWSWIRE, SEPTEMBER 28, 1992

CAN AIDS BE PREVENTED?

"I think man is responsible for his own problems. And there is a way
of escape—abstinence and monogamy. That does not mean I con-
done the type of lifestyle that might have led to AIDS. But people
who lead an exemplary life can catch AIDS, through blood transfu-
sions, passing it on to a child and many other ways. . . . We must do
everything we can to stop it."

— *THE TORONTO STAR*, OCTOBER 23, 1988

YOU'VE SAID THAT YOU'LL RETIRE WHEN GOD RETIRES YOU,
BUT DON'T THE RIGORS OF PREACHING TAKE A TOLL ON
YOUR HEALTH?

"Physically, I'm getting a little too slow and too weak to speak in
these big stadiums. . . . It takes a lot of mental effort and physical
effort to preach in a big stadium like last night. That's easier done by
a man in his 40s. Most of the well-known evangelists were dead by
the time they got to be my age, except John Wesley."

— *THE HAMILTON SPECTATOR* (ONTARIO, CANADA), JUNE 26, 1992,
DURING A FIVE-DAY CRUSADE AT PHILADELPHIA'S VETERAN'S STADIUM

YOUR HEALTH HAS BEEN EXCELLENT FOR A LONG TIME UNTIL
AROUND 1990, WHEN AT 71 YEARS OLD YOU HAD PART OF A RIB
REMOVED. YOU HAD SOME HUMOROUS COMMENTS AT THE TIME.

"I am in excellent condition, as good a shape as a man my age should
be. I have no real problem that I can feel. . . . I am recovering from
50 years of preaching, I suppose. This is the longest period I have
ever taken off, and the first real vacation I have ever had."

— *ORLANDO SENTINEL* (FLORIDA), JULY 21, 1990

HAS ILL HEALTH LED YOU TO RECOMMIT YOURSELF TO JESUS?

"I was in the hospital a lot last year, 16 weeks altogether, I think. One
night after an operation, I knew I was dying, or at least I thought I
was. Then I began to think of all the disobedience I had for my
mother and father, and all the things in my life that I could have done
better. I was in a Catholic hospital, so there was a cross on the wall.
And I thought of Jesus on the cross, and I yielded myself anew. I had
the greatest peace I've ever had in my life. And I still have it tonight."

— *ASHEVILLE CITIZEN-TIMES* (NORTH CAROLINA), OCTOBER 14, 2001

WHERE DO YOU FIND THE STRENGTH TO PREACH EVEN WHEN
YOU DON'T FEEL WELL?
"I know that God has left me on this earth as long as He has that I
might continue to preach His word, and even though I often feel
weak, He provides the strength for me to continue."

— *ASHEVILLE CITIZEN-TIMES* (NORTH CAROLINA), JUNE 23, 2001

HOW DID BEING SICK SO OFTEN TEST YOUR FAITH?
"I think that's the reason [to keep me humble] the Lord let me get
sick quite often. Because he knocked me down to teach me about my
own mortality."

— CNN'S *LARRY KING LIVE*, DECEMBER 25, 2005

IN YOUR EIGHTIES, WHAT MALADIES ARE YOU ENDURING
EVERY DAY?
"I don't feel normal. It's a neurological thing. If I tell my hand to
reach up, it's a delayed action between my brain and what happens."

— DESCRIBING HOW HE GOES NUMB OVER MOST OF HIS BODY AND
ESPECIALLY HIS FACE EVERY DAY AROUND 11 A.M.,
VENTURA COUNTY STAR (CALIFORNIA), JUNE 18, 2005

AT WHAT AGE DID YOU NOTICE THAT YOU WERE BECOMING
SICKER?
"When I reached about 80 my physical world turned upside down."

— ASSOCIATED PRESS, JUNE 16, 2005

HOW HAVE YOUR HEALTH ISSUES AFFECTED YOUR WORK?
"I've discovered I have just as much zeal for preaching the gospel as
ever, but I have had to realize that I am limited physically and must
drastically reduce my schedule."

— *THE DALLAS MORNING NEWS*, SEPTEMBER 23, 2000

BILLY GRAHAM'S PARTICIPATION IN INAUGURAL EVENTS AND CEREMONIES

Eisenhower	1953	Attended inaugural ceremony.
Johnson	1965	Attended inaugural ceremony and preached at a special inaugural day service at National City Christian Church.
Nixon	1969	Spent night of January 19 (Johnson's final night as president) at the White House and gave prayer at inaugural ceremony.
Nixon	1973	Attended inaugural ceremony and preached a special worship service in the White House.
Reagan	1981	Attended inaugural ceremony and gave a prayer and a homily at private inaugural day service, St. John's Episcopal Church.
Reagan	1985	Preached at inaugural prayer service at Washington National Cathedral.

Bush (George H. W.)	1989	Gave both invocation and benediction at inaugural ceremony.
Clinton	1993	Invited to spend night of January 19 (Bush's final night as president) at the White House and offered both invocation and benediction at inaugural ceremony.
Clinton	1997	Gave invocation at inaugural ceremony.
Bush (George W.)	2001	Invited to give invocation at inaugural ceremony.

SOURCE: BILLY GRAHAM EVANGELISTIC ASSOCIATION

On HEAVEN

ARE YOU SURE THAT YOU'RE GOING TO HEAVEN?

"My destination, I believe, is certain. It's heaven. I'm going to heaven and that's where I'll be, a few years from now, a few months from now."

— *The Charlotte Observer* (North Carolina), December 1, 1999

WHAT WILL BE YOUR FIRST QUESTION TO GOD WHEN YOU REACH HEAVEN?

"I have often said that the first thing I am going to do when I get to heaven is to ask, 'Why me, Lord? Why did you choose a farm boy from North Carolina to preach to so many people?'"

—Associated Press, September 6, 1999, citing his 1997 memoir

WHY ARE YOU LOOKING FORWARD TO DEATH AND HEAVEN?

"I'm looking forward to death. Not the process of dying, but death itself, because I know I'm going to be in the presence of Christ and everything I've ever longed for will be there."

—The Canadian Press, May 25, 1999

WHAT WILL HEAVEN BE LIKE?

"Heaven is going to be beyond even what we think about paradise. Every true believer is going to be there, and there are going to be so many people there that we'll be surprised to see. . . . And there'll be many that won't be there that we'll be surprised didn't make it."

— *HOBART MERCURY* (AUSTRALIA), JUNE 1, 1999

WHAT WILL YOU SAY TO JESUS WHEN YOU REACH HEAVEN?
"Why me? I don't deserve to be in heaven. I am a sinner. I deserve hell because I am just a sinner. But I have been saved by the grace of God through Christ. He took my sins on the cross and he died for me. You can imagine he had the most terrible sins placed upon him and he bore them because he loved us. The thought of that overwhelms me— how constant is the love and the mercy and the grace of God."

— *THE INDIANAPOLIS STAR*, MAY 30, 1999

DO YOU EVER HAVE MOMENTS OF DOUBT ABOUT GOING TO HEAVEN?
"If I were depending on myself, I would have lots of doubts, I really would, but I'm depending on Scripture. I'm not going to heaven because I'm good. I'm not going to heaven because I preached to a lot of people. I'm going to heaven because of God's grace and mercy in Christ on the cross."

— *NEWS & RECORD* (GREENSBORO, NC), SEPTEMBER 22, 1996

ARE CHILDREN AUTOMATICALLY ADMITTED TO HEAVEN?
"All the innocent children that were lost, they're not lost to God because children that young are automatically in heaven and in God's arms." *(Speaking about the children who died during the bombing of the Murrah Federal Building in Oklahoma City)*

— *DAILY NEWS* (NEW YORK), APRIL 24, 1995

IS THERE A MIDDLE GROUND BETWEEN HEAVEN AND HELL?

"You may think you are a good and upright person and that you have done nothing worthy of damnation. . . . But there's no middle ground between heaven and hell. You are either on the road to one or the other."

— *WELLAND TRIBUNE* (ONTARIO), JULY 7, 2004

HOW DO THE SCRIPTURES DESCRIBE HEAVEN?

"Oh, it's gorgeous. The twenty-first chapter of Revelation describes it in detail, no more tears, no more suffering, no more death, not even a sun or a moon, because God is the light of heaven. . . . I think there will be a lot of people. And a lot of people won't be there, too, that you expect to be there."

—MSNBC'S *HARDBALL*, MAY 29, 2006

On HIMSELF

DO YOU THINK ABOUT A SUCCESSOR?

"It seems the older I get, the more I am asked who will succeed me. Well, the fact is that I am just one of many thousands who have been called to be an evangelist. I don't need a successor, only willing hands to accept the torch I have been carrying."

— *THE DALLAS MORNING NEWS*, JULY 29, 2000

WHEN WILL YOU RETIRE?

"I do not intend to retire until God retires me."

— *BUSINESS JOURNAL* NEWSPAPER, JULY 7, 2000

"I'll be preaching to crowds as long as I can. I feel very fortunate God has spared me this long. I'm looking forward to going to heaven but also to keep serving Him right here. There aren't many 81-year-old evangelists."

— *THE COMMERCIAL APPEAL* (MEMPHIS, TN), MAY 27, 2000

WHAT DO YOU SAY TO PEOPLE WHO HAVE SAID YOU TRY TO CONVERT PEOPLE FROM OTHER RELIGIONS?

"I've never targeted a particular group. I preach the gospel and let it go where it goes. I don't target Jewish people or Muslim people."

— *THE TENNESSEAN*, JUNE 1, 2000

EARLY IN YOUR PREACHING LIFE, YOU FELT INTIMIDATED
WHEN YOU LEARNED THAT THE POWERFUL PUBLISHER HENRY
R. LUCE WAS IN THE AUDIENCE. HOW DID YOU STEEL
YOURSELF? DID GOD HELP YOU THROUGH?
"It was as if he was saying to me, 'If you pull your punches . . . I'll
make you look like a fool in front of men!'"

— *DAILY OKLAHOMAN* (OKLAHOMA CITY), OCTOBER 24, 1999

HOW WOULD YOU DESCRIBE YOUR WORK?
"I am not a professor. I am not a theologian. I'm a simple proclaimer.
You see, the word *evangelist* means an announcer. Like a newscaster
at night on the television. I am announcing the news that God loves
you and that you can be forgiven of your sins. And you can go to
heaven."

— *ST. LOUIS POST-DISPATCH* (MISSOURI), OCTOBER 10, 1999

WERE YOU SURPRISED WHEN THE GOSPEL MUSIC ASSOCIATION
WANTED TO HONOR YOU IN ITS HALL OF FAME?
"I was honored, but I told George [George Beverly Shea, who sang
during fifty years of crusades], 'Don't those people know that I can't
even sing a note?'"

— *CALGARY HERALD* (ALBERTA, CANADA), APRIL 23, 1999

WHAT HAVE BEEN YOUR PHILOSOPHY AND CONDITIONS
UNDER WHICH YOU WILL PREACH?
"I intend to go anywhere, sponsored by anybody, to preach the
Gospel of Christ, if there are no strings attached to my message. I am
sponsored by civic clubs, universities, ministerial associations, and
councils of churches all over the world."

— *OTTAWA CITIZEN*, JUNE 25, 1998

DO YOU HAVE ANY PERSONAL REGRETS?

"I should have studied more and prayed more and spent more time with my family."

— *USA TODAY*, FEBRUARY 5, 1998

DID YOU EVER THINK YOU HAD A DIFFERENT CALLING?

"I accepted God's call into the ministry on the 18th hole of a golf course where I was a caddy and met famous preachers. . . . Before that, I thought I would become a professional baseball player or a farmer, like my father."

— *THE DALLAS MORNING NEWS*, OCTOBER 22, 1998

HOW WOULD YOU LIKE TO BE REMEMBERED?

"A man that was faithful. A man that had integrity. And a man who put Christ first in his life. And a man that loved his family, loved the Church."

— *ORLANDO SENTINEL* (FLORIDA), OCTOBER 21, 1998

WHY HAVE YOU TAILORED YOUR MESSAGE TO REACH ALL DENOMINATIONS?

"I don't think it has been my doing, I think it is the doing of the Lord. I think people both inside and outside the church feel there is something missing in our lives. They're searching for that something. Whatever their ethnic background, whether they are Hispanic or African-American or whatever, there is a search for something they never find until they find God. There is an emptiness today in the hearts of many people and they don't know what it is. Entertainment doesn't satisfy them; sex doesn't satisfy; drugs don't satisfy them; materialism doesn't satisfy them. They are searching for something else."

— *ST. PETERSBURG TIMES* (FLORIDA), OCTOBER 18, 1998

WHY DID YOU CHOOSE THE TITLE *JUST AS I AM* FOR ONE OF YOUR BOOKS?

"You don't have to go and change clothes or change anything. Come like you are to God because he loves you no matter what your condition is . . . It means for me personally, that this book, I hope, tells the story of my heart, as I really am that people don't see."

— *USA TODAY*, MAY 15, 1997

WHAT IS LIFE'S BIGGEST SURPRISE FOR YOU?

"The brevity of it."

— *CALGARY HERALD* (ALBERTA, CANADA), MAY 10, 1997

HOW DO YOU HANDLE SADNESS?

"I take it to the Lord in prayer and take it to my wife, because she's the one that I confide in the most, and she confides in me, and we pray together and I just say that these things are from God, for some reason that I don't understand."

— CNN's *LARRY KING LIVE*, MAY 25, 1996

HAVE YOU EVER SMOKED?

"I can tell you I never did smoke as a habit but I did smoke one cigarette. My father caught me and he made it uncomfortable for me, and I've never had a desire since."

— *THE PATRIOT LEDGER* (QUINCY, MA), OCTOBER 26, 1996

WHY DID GOD CHOOSE YOU TO BE A PREACHER?

"Why does God choose anybody? I don't know. It's a sovereign act of God. . . . I'm still just a country boy."

— *CHATTANOOGA TIMES FREE PRESS* (TENNESSEE), SEPTEMBER 22, 1996

WHAT DOES SCRIPTURE SAY ABOUT RETIREMENT?
"I do not find any place in the Bible where anybody retires."
— *THE WASHINGTON POST*, MARCH 14, 1995

ARE YOU SOMETIMES AMAZED AT HOW FAR YOUR PREACHING
HAS GONE BOTH TECHNOLOGICALLY AND IN HOW MANY
PEOPLE YOU'VE REACHED?
"I'm just sort of the old man looking back in wonderment because
when we started out we didn't even have our own auditoriums. We
had to build our own tabernacles." *(Commenting before the Global
Mission satellite link-up that broadcast his words to more than 175 countries simultaneously)*
— *THE POST & COURIER* (CHARLESTON, SC), FEBRUARY 26, 1995

HOW WOULD YOU SUMMARIZE YOUR MISSION TO REACH
PEOPLE SUFFERING ALL OVER THE WORLD, ESPECIALLY IN
FARAWAY PLACES?
"In our message of hope, what we are trying to do is set an example
as Christians that we are doing something for them, for their physical and psychological suffering."
— *SEATTLE POST-INTELLIGENCER*, FEBRUARY 8, 1995

ARE YOU SOMETIMES ASTONISHED AT HOW LONG YOU'VE BEEN
PREACHING?
"Think of it. I've been around long enough to have preached to one-
third of the history of Southern Baptists." *(On speaking at the denomination's 150th anniversary in Atlanta)*
— *THE NEW YORK TIMES*, JUNE 24, 1995

YOU HAVE A VERY BUSY SCHEDULE, BUT WHAT DO YOU DO IN
YOUR OFF HOURS SPENT AT HOME?

"From my front porch I can see 20 miles. Ruth and I sit there in the
evening and watch the lightning bugs. . . . We sit there with our dogs
and cat and hold hands and talk about our children. We talk about
the Lord, how wonderful he is. And we thank God we have that
place."

— *THE ATLANTA JOURNAL AND CONSTITUTION*, OCTOBER 9, 1994

HOW WOULD YOU SUM UP THE LEGACY THAT YOU WOULD
LIKE TO LEAVE?

"I think that any legacy will be in the lives and the hearts of the
people, as the Apostle Paul indicated, whose lives have been irrevo-
cably changed in these various ministries and also in the evangelists
we have helped to train and on the new emphasis on evangelism in
various denominations. I hope our ministry has made a difference for
the good in the church and for the Kingdom of God."

— *PLAIN DEALER* (CLEVELAND, OHIO), MAY 22, 1994

MANY PEOPLE CLAIM VISIONS OF GOD OR CHRIST. HAVE YOU
EVER SEEN SUCH VISIONS?

"I've never seen a vision of God or Christ. It's never happened to me.
I'm sure that there may be people who have had that experience."

— *CHICAGO TRIBUNE*, MAY 1, 1994

WHAT'S THE MISTAKE THAT'S BEEN THE HARDEST FOR YOU TO
LIVE WITH?

"Not studying enough. I don't think anybody considers me an intellectual or a very smart man. I'm just an ordinary man. I feel more like
a plowboy back on the farm today than I ever did."

—ABC NEWS, *PRIMETIME LIVE*, DECEMBER 30, 1993

DO YOU EVER GET ANGRY AT PEOPLE?

"I don't get mad at people and I don't write ugly things or say ugly things. My staff thinks I'm too easygoing. But I'm like Will Rogers. I never met anybody I didn't like."

— *THE TORONTO STAR*, AUGUST 15, 1987

DO YOU EVER FEEL OVERWHELMED, THAT MAYBE YOUR WORK DIDN'T TURN OUT THE WAY YOU WANTED IT TO?

"To be honest with you, there are too many times when I feel I'm preaching from an empty well. Really, I feel far more humble now than when I began 40 years ago. You take my upcoming Washington Crusade. The numbers don't really matter, do they? And what can you really hope to accomplish in eight days? If just one person changes his ways because of me, then maybe in God's sight I'll be a success. Forty years ago, I thought I was going to change the whole world. I don't think that anymore. You know, Jesus was here only three years with his public life. He went about from town to town. And then he said, 'I have finished the work the Father has given me to do.'"

— *THE WASHINGTON POST*, APRIL 28, 1986

WHEN WILL YOU KNOW IF YOUR ACCOMPLISHMENTS WERE SUCCESSFUL OR NOT?

"What good my ministry has done I'll never know until I get to heaven. Then I may find that some obscure preacher working in a slum mission somewhere has done more to advance the kingdom of God than I."

— *SATURDAY EVENING POST*, MARCH, 1986

WHAT DREAMS DID YOU HAVE WHEN YOU WERE YOUNG?

"There were two people I didn't want to be when I grew up—one was a clergyman and the other was an undertaker. I always wanted to be a baseball player."

—UNITED PRESS INTERNATIONAL, MAY 19, 1985

HAVE YOU PAID A PERSONAL PRICE FOR YOUR MINISTRY?
"Cost? How could I say that it has cost me anything? In fact, it has cost me too little. The Apostle Paul was beaten and stoned and put in jail to follow Christ and I'd hate to go to heaven with no stripes, no scars."

—ASSOCIATED PRESS, MAY 1, 1982

YOU'VE SAID THAT IF YOU HAD IT TO DO OVER AGAIN, YOU WOULD HAVE SPENT MORE TIME IN STUDY AND PRAYER AND LESS TIME TRAVELING, SPENT MORE TIME IN ONE PLACE. WHY?
"I think I went to too many places throughout the world, and I would have stayed longer in different cities as a way of building up. People have become convicted of their sins, and they're ready to turn to Christ after they've come several nights instead of just one night."

—*THE DALLAS MORNING NEWS*, OCTOBER 12, 2002

HAVE YOU EVER CONSIDERED A DIFFERENT VOCATION?
"You could not offer me a job as an ambassador or a Cabinet post that I would give a second thought to. When God called me to preach, it was for life."

—*THE CINCINNATI ENQUIRER*, JUNE 23, 2002,
CITING RUSS BUSBY'S BOOK *BILLY GRAHAM: GOD'S AMBASSADOR*

HOW HAVE YOUR IDEAS ABOUT HUMAN RIGHTS CHANGED OVER THE YEARS?
"I am now an old man of 83 suffering from several ailments. As I reflect back, I realize that much of my life has been a pilgrimage—constantly learning, changing, growing and maturing. I have come to see in deeper ways some of the implications of my faith and message, not the least of which is in the area of human rights and racial and ethnic understanding."

—PART OF AN OPEN LETTER APOLOGIZING FOR ANTI-JEWISH REMARKS DISCOVERED
DURING THE OPENING OF THE NIXON TAPES, *THE JEWISH WEEK*, MARCH 22, 2002

WERE YOU SURPRISED THAT YOU WERE ASKED TO PREACH
WELL INTO YOUR 80S?

"To be honest, I never expected to continue receiving invitations into
my 80s." *(After being asked to preach in San Diego)*

— *THE CHRISTIAN CENTURY*, FEBRUARY 8, 2003

DO YOU LIKE TO RETURN TO PLACES THAT YOU'VE PREACHED
BEFORE?

"I feel somewhat like the Apostle Paul in wanting to go back to
places where we have preached the Lord to see how they are doing.
More important, however, there is a new generation that needs to
hear the Gospel since our last crusade there in 1985."

— WHEN THE GREATER LOS ANGELES CRUSADE WAS ANNOUNCED
MONTHS EARLIER, BUSINESS WIRE, NOVEMBER 24, 2004

DO YOU VIEW YOURSELF AS A RIGHTEOUS PERSON?

"I think I'm just a sinner saved by the grace of God."

— RELIGION NEWS SERVICE, NOVEMBER 22, 2004

YOU'VE SAID THAT PART OF YOUR MOTIVATION TO CONTINUE
PREACHING IS TO OFFER POSITIVE ALTERNATIVES TO YOUTH
INSTEAD OF WHAT THEY CURRENTLY SEE IN MOVIES AND ON
TELEVISION. WHAT'S YOUR OPINION OF THE CURRENT
ENTERTAINMENT ENVIRONMENT?

"The entertainment industry has put out such extreme, extremely
shallow things and vicious things. I've seen ads of some of these
motion pictures and it's very disturbing if you are a parent."

— CITY NEWS SERVICE, NOVEMBER 18, 2004

WHAT WERE YOUR TWO MOST IMPORTANT RELIGIOUS EXPERIENCES?

"I was reared in the church, in the Presbyterian Church. And I went faithfully to church, but I didn't get anything out of it. I just sat there, because my parents insisted, of course, that I go. And when I was about sixteen or seventeen, an evangelist came to our town. And he attracted a lot of people, and out of curiosity, I was taken by one of the people who worked for my father on the dairy farm. He took me to the meetings, and I listened to him. He gave an invitation to receive Christ and to change your life, and I responded, and it did change my life. I had a new view of everything. And then later, on a golf course in Florida, I felt called to preach the gospel. And one night in the full moon and the palm trees around where our school was, I knelt down there alone. And I said, 'Lord, I'll do what you want me to do and go where you want me to go,' and that was another big spiritual experience for me."

—CNN's *LARRY KING LIVE*, DECEMBER 25, 2005

DO YOU HAVE ANY WORRIES ABOUT THE WORLD THAT YOU WILL LEAVE BEHIND WHEN YOU DIE?

"The world we leave behind is about like the world was when I came into the world just at the end of World War I. And the world was at each other's throats at that time. And thousands were being killed. Today, we don't have a world war, but maybe we do in terrorism. But man's heart is the same. I don't see any difference in people's hearts."

—*NBC NIGHTLY NEWS*, JUNE 24, 2005

YOU'VE SAID ON A NUMBER OF OCCASIONS THAT YOU CONSIDER YOURSELF A FAILURE. WHY IS THAT?

"I feel that if I had stayed home more, studied more, I would have done more for God and my soul. I needed to grow inside more. I traveled too much, went on too many places, accepted too many invitations, not only to speak but just to be at a social or something like that. And I needed to be preparing so that when I do come and talk to a person that he sense something is coming to him that is supernatural."

—CNN's *LARRY KING LIVE*, MAY 29, 2005

WHY DID YOU HEED GOD'S CALL TO BE A PREACHER?

"I never wanted to be a preacher; I never wanted to be anything in the Church. But I told God that I will be what you want me to be, and I will do what you want me to do—that was my call. In just over one week I will be 80 years old. I continue to go on and on, and that call has never left."

—PR NEWSWIRE, OCTOBER 26, 1998

THE GRAHAM FAMILY

William (Billy) F. Graham
Married: Ruth McCue Bell
Children: Virginia, 1945
        Anne Morrow, 1948
        Ruth Bell, 1950
        William Franklin, III, 1952
        Nelson Edman, 1958
19 grandchildren, numerous great-grandchildren

SOURCE: BILLY GRAHAM EVANGELISTIC ASSOCIATION

On His Family

HOW WOULD YOU DESCRIBE YOUR SON WILLIAM FRANKLIN
GRAHAM III?

"There are some that think my son, Franklin, may someday be the
man. He has his own organization, which he had built from scratch.
He is a very powerful speaker and Bible teacher and very authorita-
tive in the pulpit. He has a presence about him."

— *THE NEW YORK TIMES*, NOVEMBER 10, 1981

WILL FRANKLIN BE SUCCESSFUL?

"I know Franklin has the ability, the energy and the background to
do almost anything in Christian work. He'll have my all-out support
whichever direction he chooses to go as long as he's true and faithful to God. . . . I don't expect him to follow exactly in my footsteps.
He'll develop his own vision. He'll be his own man. I don't intend
to interfere."

— *THE NEWS AND OBSERVER* (RALEIGH, NC), DECEMBER 26, 1999

HOW DO YOU RATE FRANKLIN AS A PREACHER?

"I've listened to him preach by tape and in person and he's a far better preacher than I am now."

—NBC's *SUNDAY TODAY*, MAY 10, 1998

DO YOU AND FRANKLIN HAVE DIFFERENT PREACHING STYLES?
"Franklin and I preach the same gospel, he just approaches it differently. He is not a clone."

— *THE ALBUQUERQUE TRIBUNE* (NEW MEXICO), MAY 9, 1998

YOUR MOTHER, MRS. MORROW COFFEY GRAHAM, DIED AT EIGHTY-NINE AFTER AN ILLNESS OF SEVERAL MONTHS, AND YOU WERE BY HER SIDE WHEN SHE PASSED. YOU'VE SAID, "SHE WAS A WOMAN WHO HAS PREACHED SOME OF THE BEST SERMONS I HAVE EVER HEARD IN MY LIFE." HOW ELSE WOULD YOU CHARACTERIZE HER LIFE AND HER FAITH?
"She knew the Bible like few women in Charlotte, and she lived very close to what she knew."

—UNITED PRESS INTERNATIONAL, AUGUST 15, 1981

YOU WERE AWAY A LOT DURING YOUR CRUSADES; DO YOU WISH YOU HAD SPENT MORE TIME AT HOME WITH YOUR FAMILY?
"If I had it to do over, I would stay home more. But I was home maybe 30 percent of the time, maybe 35 percent of the time, even in the busiest times."

— *THE FLORIDA TIMES-UNION* (JACKSONVILLE), NOVEMBER 2, 2000

ANY OTHER REGRETS ABOUT YOUR FAMILY?
"I've neglected them. I've traveled too much, written too many articles, written too many books." (*On turning seventy-nine and making the decision to stay home more with his family*)

—*HARTFORD COURANT* (CONNECTICUT), SEPTEMBER 7, 1998

ON MANY OCCASIONS YOU'VE PUBLICLY PROCLAIMED YOUR
LOVE FOR YOUR WIFE, RUTH, ESPECIALLY ON HER EIGHTIETH
BIRTHDAY. WHAT DID YOU SAY TO HER?

"You could see Christ coming out of her face in the expression she
had. My dear Ruth. You have been more than I could ever have
dreamed."

—ASSOCIATED PRESS STATE & LOCAL WIRE, MAY 31, 2000, AT HIS WIFE'S
EIGHTIETH BIRTHDAY GALA AND HOSPITAL FUND-RAISER IN ASHEVILLE

WHAT'S THE SECRET TO YOUR LONG MARRIAGE?

"I have a remarkable wife who has dedicated her life to being my
helpmate. We decided that she would raise the family, and I would
go and preach the Gospel."

—*ORLANDO SENTINEL* (FLORIDA), NOVEMBER 4, 1996

YOU'RE PROUD OF ALL YOUR CHILDREN, BUT WHY DO YOU
CALL ANNE A MIRACLE?

"She is a miracle of God . . . because she never went beyond high
school. How she ever got to where she is I have no idea, but she's
invited to countries all over the world and to theological schools and
seminaries to lecture and to speak. She has a greater knowledge of the
Bible by far than I do. She'd get up early in the morning to pray and
read the Scriptures. Now she's a walking Bible encyclopedia."

—*THE CHARLOTTE OBSERVER* (NORTH CAROLINA), SEPTEMBER 22, 1996

HOW IS GOD USING FRANKLIN AND HIS CHARITY,
SAMARITAN'S PURSE?

"I think God is really using him—not only to preach the Gospel, but
also in social work around the world. He is on the cutting edge of
helping people in the hot spots of the world."

—ASSOCIATED PRESS, AUGUST 26, 1994

YOU OWE A LOT TO RUTH, DON'T YOU?

"I think we all owe a debt of gratitude to your mother for putting up with me for 50 years and then taking you on." *(Said to Franklin in jest before a crowd attending a revival in Charleston, West Virginia)*

— *CHARLESTON DAILY MAIL* (WEST VIRGINIA), APRIL 30, 1994

YOU TRUSTED GOD TO HELP RUTH RAISE THE CHILDREN. HOW SO?

"I hated it . . . leaving my children. But it was my call from God. It took precedence over everything. It still does. I trusted the Lord that Ruth would raise them right."

— *SUN-SENTINEL* (FORT LAUDERDALE, FL), AUGUST 15, 1993

WHAT IS THE SECRET OF A LONG AND HAPPY MARRIAGE?

"We have had our share of joy and heartache over these past 50 years, but through it all, our love and faith in one another and in our Lord has enabled us to face whatever challenge has been placed before us." *(On celebrating 50 years of marriage)*

— *ST. PETERSBURG TIMES* (FLORIDA), AUGUST 14, 1993

HOW HAS RUTH BEEN INSTRUMENTAL TO YOUR CALLING?

"Without her love for the Lord and for me and her dedication to evangelism, I would not have been able to function for the Lord as I have. When one partner is away from home as much as I have been, it is both a honeymoon and a readjustment period every time we get back together. Ruth's knowledge of the Bible, sense of humor and her shared commitment to my ministry have been an anchor in our marriage."

— PR NEWSWIRE, AUGUST 6, 1993

WHO IS THE LEADER IN YOUR MARRIAGE?
"Ephesians 5 describes a relationship of trust, love, intimacy and organization in marriage which is important and has been terribly misunderstood and abused. . . . The husband is the head of the wife just as Christ is the head of the Church, implies leadership. Some husbands won't take leadership. The wife has to do it. . . . I was away a great deal. My wife had to be the leader."

— *THE POST-STANDARD* (SYRACUSE, NY), APRIL 29, 1989

WAS YOUR PREACHING A BURDEN FOR RUTH IN WAYS OTHER THAN YOU BEING AWAY A GREAT DEAL?
"It's not been an easy life for Ruth . . . to have your privacy intruded upon constantly, to answer the phone hundreds of times a week, to be interviewed and photographed, which she dreads."

—ASSOCIATED PRESS, JUNE 9, 1981

YOU'VE TRIED TO STEER CLEAR OF SOME OF THE CONTROVERSIAL STATEMENTS YOUR SON FRANKLIN SAID ABOUT ISLAM BEING A "WICKED" RELIGION. HOW DID YOU HANDLE THIS TOUCHY SITUATION?
"I'm not going to get into these topics. I'm coming for one reason only, to tell about the love of God in Christ. And there will be all kinds of theological backgrounds there. And I welcome them, and I love them."

— *THE DALLAS MORNING NEWS,* OCTOBER 8, 2002

WERE YOU SURPRISED WHEN YOUR BROTHER, MELVIN, DIED BEFORE YOU, A DAY BEFORE HIS SEVENTY-NINTH BIRTHDAY?
"Melvin was snatched straight into the presence of Jesus. Melvin is already there. I'm almost envious of him. I certainly expected I'd be there before him."

— *THE NEWS & OBSERVER* (RALEIGH, NC), AUGUST 30, 2003

HAS YOUR MARRIAGE GOTTEN BETTER WITH TIME?

"We have a better relationship now. We look into each other's eyes and touch each other. It gets better as you get older. The secret is the Lord Christ—to have him in the center of our lives."

—THE ASSOCIATED PRESS STATE, AUGUST 14, 2003

On HUMOR

"People ask me, 'Isn't this your last crusade?' They say it very hopefully, some of them."

— *U.S. NEWS & WORLD REPORT*, DECEMBER 23, 2002

"It has my name on the back and I'm No. 1. I may show up at the next game and see where they put me." *(Joking about a Dallas Cowboys jersey given to him by the team)*

—ASSOCIATED PRESS, OCTOBER 15, 2002

"There are more marriages than divorces, which proves that preachers can still out-talk lawyers."

— *MONTEREY COUNTY HERALD* (CALIFORNIA), NOVEMBER 6, 2003

"God loves you and so do I. And I love all of you. I wish I could come home with you and visit with you and have a cup of tea or coffee with you, but it's impossible. But we'll do it in heaven, and we can make appointments and spend five years together."

—TO A CROWD OF ABOUT 7,750 PEOPLE NEAR THE CONCLUSION
OF THE HEART OF AMERICA CRUSADE IN ARROWHEAD STADIUM,
KANSAS, MISSOURI, *THE TOPEKA CAPITAL-JOURNAL* (KANSAS), OCTOBER 10, 2004

"I look forward to death. I look forward to seeing God face-to-face. I hope I'll see all of you [reporters] there. And bring your cameras."

— *CHICAGO TRIBUNE*, JUNE 26, 2005

"They came out with headlines when I was in Houston once—I think it was the *Chronicle*—that I was running for president or something like that. And so some people had called and said they'd give me their delegates at the convention, and I forget whether it was Democratic or Republican now. But my wife had seen it on television. She called and said they'll never elect a divorced man, which is what I would be if I did this."

— CNN's *AMERICAN MORNING*, JUNE 23, 2005

"Don't get old, if you can avoid it." *(Said while apologizing to a visitor for not getting up because of his infirmities)*

— *PEOPLE*, JUNE 20, 2005

BILLY GRAHAM'S RESPONSE WHEN ASKED BY A CYNIC HOW HE KNEW GOD EXISTED:
"Well, that's an easy one . . . because I spoke with him this morning."

— *HERALD EXPRESS* (TORQUAY), FEBRUARY 4, 2006

ON A STROLL IN NEW YORK CITY, BILLY GRAHAM WAS APPROACHED BY SOMEONE WHO SHOUTED: "GIVE 'EM HELL, BILLY."
Graham responded, "I'm not going to give 'em hell; I'm going to give 'em heaven."

WHEN HE REALIZED THAT HIS BOOK *HOPE FOR THE TROUBLED HEART* HAD BEEN GIVEN TO GUESTS AT A LUNCHEON OF BROADCASTERS AND PUBLISHERS AT ABC HEADQUARTERS, WHERE GRAHAM RECEIVED THE LOWELL THOMAS AWARD FOR DISTINGUISHED ACHIEVEMENT, HE REMARKED:

"If I'd known you were going to do this, I'd have done a better job with it."

—ASSOCIATED PRESS, SEPTEMBER 20, 1991

WHAT JOKE DO YOU LIKE TO TELL ABOUT RESPECTING AND UNDERSTANDING DIFFERENT RELIGIONS?

"A Baptist preacher visited a racetrack and refused to gamble until he saw a Catholic priest blessing horses before the start of each race. Four consecutive times the priest blessed the horse that went on to win. Finally the preacher convinced himself that it wouldn't be gambling to bet on a sure thing, so he put all his money on the horse the priest blessed only to see the horse drop dead halfway through the race.

"So the preacher went to the priest and said, 'Father, what happened? You blessed four consecutive horses and they won. But you blessed that one and the horse dropped dead.'

"The priest said, 'Well, you mustn't be a Catholic, otherwise you would have known the difference between a blessing and the last rites.'"

—*CHICAGO TRIBUNE*, APRIL 20, 1988

"I came into town the night before last and I saw the signs all over town that said Graham, Graham, Graham, and I thought 'My, they've done a good job. Then I looked at the small letters and they all said 'Bob.'" *(Told during the election season in which Florida governor Bob Graham was running)*

—ASSOCIATED PRESS, OCTOBER 31, 1986

On MONEY AND MATERIAL WEALTH

HOW CAN MONEY STAND IN THE WAY OF SALVATION?

"Money can buy a bed, but not sleep; finery, not beauty; a house, not a home; books, but not an education; medicine, but not health; religion, but not salvation. Money and material things can be an obstacle to reaching Christ."

— *ST. LOUIS POST-DISPATCH* (MISSOURI), OCTOBER 16, 1999

HAVE PEOPLE THROUGHOUT THE AGES BEEN RUINED BY THE LOVE OF MONEY?

"Money is the root of all evil, the Bible says—the love of money. And we've become so greedy that we're willing to damn people's souls and destroy their lives for money. And that's been true throughout history. It's not just today; it's yesterday and tomorrow and from now on." *(On entertainment media that shows excessive violence)*

—CNN'S *LARRY KING LIVE*, APRIL 28, 1999

CAN WE BE SATISFIED BY MONEY ALONE?

"Our hearts aren't satisfied by materialism. They can't be. That's why you see someone who has made millions driven on to make more millions. People confuse amassing money with security. But it is not so. What a pity to confuse real security with making money."

— *PARADE* MAGAZINE, OCTOBER 20, 1997

HOW DO YOU EXPLAIN THE ALLURE OF MONEY AND MATERIAL GOODS IF ITS ACQUISITION DOESN'T MAKE US SATISFIED?
"It's ironic that with all the attempts to achieve happiness, people have found everything but happiness. . . . There's the escape of pleasure, into passion, appetites and desire, sexual fantasies, escape into drugs and alcohol. You think, 'If I could just have that drug—or vodka, or that girl in bed with me'—but it doesn't work that way. It doesn't give you peace, joy or satisfaction. It doesn't fill that void, and millions have that void that needs to be filled."

— *SAN ANTONIO EXPRESS-NEWS* (TEXAS), APRIL 9, 1997,

DURING A SOUTH TEXAS CRUSADE

WHAT DID JESUS SAY ABOUT RICHES AND YOUR SOUL?
"Jesus said if you had it all it's not compared to one soul—you. Your soul is you. You may own the whole world and wake up one morning and find yourself missing the most important thing—your soul."

— *THE CHARLOTTE OBSERVER* (NORTH CAROLINA), SEPTEMBER 28, 1996

CAN MONEY SOLVE OUR PROBLEMS?
"We in America have got the idea . . . that all we have to do is vote some more money and that'll solve any problem. It takes away our own personal involvement, our own personal responsibility. . . . Just go to a committee meeting. Get organized in an air-conditioned room, vote some more money. . . . Go home and forget it, and the race problem is solved and the welfare problem is solved and the social conditions will be better."

— *THE COLUMBUS DISPATCH* (OHIO), JUNE 5, 1993

WHAT IS YOUR VIEW ON PUBLIC AND PRIVATE DEBT?

"We must do all we can do to get rid of debt. We have to focus more on the infrastructures and the people in our major cities."

— *THE PHILADELPHIA TRIBUNE*, JUNE 26, 1992

DOES SCRIPTURE TELL US THAT YOU CAN'T TAKE IT WITH YOU WHEN YOU DIE?

"Solomon had it all, and at the end of his life, he said, 'It's not worth it . . . Vanity of vanities, all is vanity.' Riches fly away as an eagle. . . . Have you ever seen a hearse going to the graveyard with a U-Haul-It truck behind it carrying the fellow's goods?" *(Quoting Scripture about Solomon's wealth and its relation to modern times)*

— *ARKANSAS DEMOCRAT-GAZETTE* (LITTLE ROCK), SEPTEMBER 19, 1989

WHAT ARE THE PITFALLS OF NEWFOUND ECONOMIC PROGRESS?

"All too often economic progress and expanded freedom have been accompanied by moral and spiritual decay, leading to a host of social ills such as alcoholism, drug abuse, disintegration of families, loneliness, crime and lack of compassion for others. . . . The issues which face our world are fundamentally moral and spiritual, and they cannot be satisfied by economic or political solutions alone. How tragic it would be if Hungary fell into the same trap as many in my own country, and gained the whole world, but lost its soul. Material progress is important, but it can make us forget God and his will for our lives." *(During a crusade in Hungary)*

— *LOS ANGELES TIMES*, JULY 29, 1989

DO WE PLACE TOO MUCH HOPE IN TECHNOLOGY TO MAKE
OUR LIVES BETTER?

"Materialism has not brought the deep sense of satisfaction that many
people are searching for. We thought technology would save time,
and we're busier than ever."

—PR NEWSWIRE EUROPE, JUNE 1, 1989

WHAT IS ONE WAY FOR INDIVIDUALS TO COMBAT FALSE
PREACHERS?

"There's power in the Gospel, even if it's quoted by the devil. . . . I
know people that have come to Christ under the preaching of someone who was totally false. . . . [Even so,] we have a responsibility not
to send money to people who are false."

—*NEWSDAY* (NEW YORK), MAY 12, 1988

YOU HAVE ESTABLISHED A SYSTEM WHERE YOU DON'T NEED
CONTRIBUTIONS TO KEEP YOUR WORK GOING, SO YOUR
CRUSADES ARE NOT ABOUT SOLICITING MONEY, AND YOU
RAISE MOST OF YOUR MONEY THROUGH OTHER AVENUES.
WHEN DID YOU MAKE THIS DECISION?

"Early on. I've always said if I have to plead for money or beg for
money, I would quit."

—*LOS ANGELES TIMES*, APRIL 25, 1987

WHAT QUESTION DID YOU ASK IN THE EARLY 1960S THAT
STILL RINGS TRUE TODAY AS FAR AS MONEY AND RELIGION
ARE CONCERNED?

"The great question of our time is, will we be motivated by materialistic philosophy or by spiritual power?"

—DURING A NINETEEN-DAY CRUSADE IN SOLDIER FIELD, BOSTON, IN JUNE 1962,
CITED BY *LEXINGTON HERALD LEADER* (KENTUCKY), JUNE 29, 2005

WHAT WAS THE GREATEST LESSON TO BE LEARNED FROM
HURRICANE KATRINA?

"That there is much more to life than material things. There is a
moral and spiritual strength needed—not only in New Orleans and
the Lower Ninth Ward, but everywhere. We are living through a very
tumultuous period of history, including the aftereffects of Hurricane
Katrina and the war in Iraq. If ever the world needed to turn to God,
it is now."

—PR NEWSWIRE, MARCH 10, 2006

On MORALITY

WHAT IS THE IMPORTANCE OF KEEPING A MORAL HOME?
"No place in the New Testament does it say we are supposed to pursue happiness. There is a satanic attack today on the home as I have never seen before. When we lose the home, we lose the country."

—UNITED PRESS INTERNATIONAL, JULY 30, 1981

YOU HAVE CALLED FOR ALL EVANGELISTS TO DISCLOSE THEIR
FINANCIAL STATEMENTS. WHY?
"A lack of financial integrity on the part of one of us can hurt the whole of the evangelical cause. We must have the highest standards in morality, ethics and integrity if we are to continue to have influence. . . . With heightened visibility has come great opportunity such as we have never had before and may never have again. But along with the great opportunities facing us as evangelicals today, there are many dangers."

—ASSOCIATED PRESS, JANUARY 28, 1981, CITING A SPEECH GIVEN AT THE NATIONAL
ASSOCIATION OF EVANGELICALS (NAE) AND THE NATIONAL RELIGIOUS
BROADCASTERS (NRB) JOINT ANNUAL CONVENTION IN WASHINGTON, DC

HOW CAN WE ACHIEVE THE MORAL HIGH GROUND?
"Something has happened to our moral life. The bottom has dropped out, and we need a revival. We need Jesus to be lifted up. . . . There's

a tremendous hunger for something to believe in, especially young people."

—*THE TENNESSEAN*, JUNE 2, 2000

HOW WAS MORALITY TAUGHT TO YOU WHEN YOU WERE YOUNG?

"I grew up in the South, and church was a big thing in our lives. I suppose it was throughout the country. In the schools, ministers were brought in to preach sermons, and the Bible was read every day. We had prayer in high school classes. This helped mold my character and my thinking. I knew some things were wrong and some things were right. We've lost that."

—ASSOCIATED PRESS, DECEMBER 17, 1999

IS CARING FOR THE ENVIRONMENT AKIN TO A MORAL ACT?

"When we abuse the environment, we pay a price. And when we break God's moral and spiritual laws, we pay a price."

—*ST. PAUL PIONEER PRESS* (MINNESOTA), JUNE 21, 1996

IN 1949, AN EIGHT-WEEK YOUTH FOR CHRIST RALLY IN LOS ANGELES WAS SO POPULAR THAT HOLLYWOOD PRODUCERS WANTED TO CAST YOU AS A LEADING MAN. WHAT WAS YOUR RESPONSE TO THEM?

"I laughed in their faces. I wouldn't do it for a million dollars a month. . . . Hollywood has done more to bring about the moral deterioration of America than any other single factor."

—*ST. PAUL PIONEER PRESS* (MINNESOTA), JUNE 13, 1996

HOW HAS YOUR ORGANIZATION HANDLED ITS FINANCES TO
BE ABOVE REPROACH?

"From the very beginning, we decided how we were going to handle
money . . . and things like that. We had seen other people fall as a
result of that, and God gave us some examples to see and to teach
us lessons." *(On being open and transparent in business and money
dealings)*

— *THE CHARLOTTE OBSERVER* (NORTH CAROLINA), SEPTEMBER 23, 1996

AFTER THE TRAGEDY OF THE MURRAH FEDERAL OFFICE
BUILDING IN OKLAHOMA CITY, YOU WERE ASKED MANY TIMES
HOW GOD COULD HAVE ALLOWED SUCH A THING TO HAPPEN.
YOU USED THE OPPORTUNITY TO DISCUSS EVIL. HOW DID YOU
CHARACTERIZE EVIL?

"There is something about evil that we will never fully understand
this side of eternity. But the Bible says two other things that we
sometimes are tempted to forget. It tells us that Satan is real and that
'He was a murderer from the beginning.' And it also tells us that the
human heart is capable of almost limitless evil when it is cut off from
God and from the moral law."

— *KNOXVILLE NEWS-SENTINEL* (TENNESSEE), APRIL 29, 1995

WHAT DOES IT MEAN TO LIVE WITH INTEGRITY?

"Living with integrity means rediscovering our direction in life, not
just increasing our speed. Integrity permeates the fabric of a person,
rather than just decorating the surface."

—PR NEWSWIRE, JANUARY 10, 1994, CITING THE MISSION '94 CRUSADE IN TOKYO

HOW HAVE YOU BEEN ABLE TO HANDLE TEMPTATIONS OF THE
FLESH, ESPECIALLY THOSE BEHAVIORS THAT HAVE SUNK OTHER
HIGH-PROFILE EVANGELISTS?

"I'm sure I've been tempted, especially in my younger days. But there
has never been anything close to an accident. . . . From the earliest
days, I've never had a meal alone with a woman other than my wife,
not even in a restaurant. I've never ridden in an automobile with
another woman."

— *SUNDAY MAIL*, NOVEMBER 17, 1991

IS IT A COINCIDENCE THAT OTHER CLERGYMEN WERE
BROUGHT DOWN BY THEIR SINS?

"I think we are living in an age when Satan is out to destroy families
. . . and I think particularly he is attacking clergy."

— *LOS ANGELES TIMES*, SEPTEMBER 21, 1991

UNLIKE SOME OTHER HIGH-PROFILE EVANGELISTS, YOU HAVE
MANAGED TO RESIST TEMPTATION AND STAY ON THE STRAIGHT
AND NARROW. TO WHAT DO YOU ATTRIBUTE YOUR SUCCESS?

"From the very beginning of my career, I was frightened—I still am
—that I would do something to dishonor the Lord."

— *TIME* MAGAZINE, NOVEMBER 14, 1988

DOES MORALITY CHANGE BASED ON WHERE WE ARE AND
WHAT WE ARE DOING?

"A man of integrity can be trusted and is the same man in his hotel
room thousands of miles from home as he is in church. Our greatest
need is moral integrity."

— SPEAKING BEFORE THE NATIONAL RELIGIOUS BROADCASTERS
ABOUT THE REVELATIONS OF SEX AND BLACKMAIL
BY TELEVANGELISTS, STATES NEWS SERVICE, FEBRUARY 2, 1988

DO TELEVANGELIST SCANDALS HAVE A WIDER MESSAGE FOR US?

"I cringe at so much suffering and immorality, the fraud and all the things going on. The biggest problem facing America is the moral situation, the scandals in business, Wall Street, sports, in every area, even the church. . . . In its own backhanded way, I think it may help the church. It has caused everybody to realize there must be financial accountability."

—*LOS ANGELES TIMES*, DECEMBER 19, 1987

HIGHLIGHTS OF BILLY GRAHAM'S LIFE

Nov. 7, 1918:   William Franklin Graham is born in
                  Charlotte, North Carolina, to a family of
                  dairy farmers.

1934:   He is saved during a Charlotte revival led by
                  evangelist Mordecai Ham.

1936:   He graduates from high school and works
                  during the summer as a door-to-door sales-
                  man for the Fuller Brush company.

March 1938:   On the golf course of Florida Bible Institute
                  (now Trinity College), he hears God's call to
                  the ministry.

1938:   While in college, he begins as a substitute
                  preacher at area churches. He is later
                  ordained a Southern Baptist minister.

1940:   Graham graduates from Florida Bible
                  Institute (now Trinity College) in Tampa,
                  Florida.

1943:   He receives a bachelor of arts degree from
                  Wheaton College in Wheaton, Illinois,
                  majoring in anthropology.

1943:   He marries Ruth McCue Bell, the daughter
                  of missionaries. They eventually have five
                  children: Virginia, Anne Morrow, Ruth Bell,
                  William Franklin, and Nelson Edman.

1943–45:   Graham is pastor of First Baptist Church in
                  Western Springs, Illinois.

Oct. 27, 1944:	Mr. Graham preaches at his first mass evangelism meeting, a Youth for Christ rally in Chicago. They ask him to work full-time for the group, and he becomes vice president from 1945 to 1948.
1947–52:	He is president of Northwestern Schools, a liberal arts college, Bible school, and seminary in Minneapolis. At the school he meets George Beverly Shea and Cliff Barrows, who become the core of his evangelistic team.
1949:	Graham's Los Angeles crusade, The Canvas Cathedral, is supposed to run for three weeks but goes for eight after newspaper publisher William Randolph Hearst tells his editors to "Puff Graham," which means to write laudatory articles. Graham receives national exposure.
1950:	Graham establishes the Billy Graham Evangelistic Association. He begins his weekly *Hour of Decision* radio show, which is heard on more than six hundred stations worldwide.
1952:	Graham begins a syndicated newspaper column, My Answer.
1953:	Graham publishes his first book, *Peace with God*.
1953:	Mr. Graham conducts a four-week crusade at the Cotton Bowl in Dallas. More than seventy-five-thousand people attend the last night.

1954:	The Grahams buy 150 acres in the remote wooded hills near Montreat, North Carolina, to build a log home.
1955:	The Gallup Poll lists Graham as one of the Ten Most Admired Men in the World. He has been listed forty-three times, more than any other individual.
1957:	Graham's four-month New York campaign is televised.
1960:	Graham does an eight-week, sixteen-city tour of nine African countries, then visits Jordan and Israel.
1965:	President Lyndon Johnson and the First Lady attend a Graham crusade in Houston.
1968:	Graham becomes the unofficial chaplain for the Nixon White House.
1982:	Graham takes his crusade to Russia, a controversial mission.
Oct. 15, 1989:	A star with his name is placed on the Hollywood Walk of Fame.
July 1992:	Graham learns that he has Parkinson's disease.
March 1995:	His Global Mission in Puerto Rico reaches an audience of one billion in 185 countries via television, videotape, and satellite.
April 1995:	He speaks at a prayer service in Oklahoma City four days after the bombing of the Alfred Murrah Federal Building.
June 1995:	Graham collapses during a speech in Toronto. He is released from a hospital three days later

	after treatment for a bleeding colon. Graham is diagnosed with prostate cancer.
Nov. 1995:	Graham breaks several ribs after falling in the shower.
May 1996:	Graham receives the Congressional Gold Medal.
Apr. 1997:	Graham's autobiography, *Just as I Am*, is published.
June 2001:	Graham's Louisville crusade attracts 191,500 people in four days.
Sept. 14, 2001:	Graham preaches at the National Day of Prayer and Remembrance following the terrorist attacks in New York and Washington.
Nov. 14, 2001:	His son Franklin is elected president of the BGEA.
July 24, 2002:	The BGEA announces that it plans to buy property in Charlotte for its new headquarters, which had been in Minneapolis.
June 17–20, 2004:	The Heart of America Crusade in Kansas City, Missouri.
June 24–26, 2005:	Graham leads the Greater New York City Crusade. The BGEA later announces that it probably will be his last crusade.

On OTHER RELIGIONS

IS THERE EVER A PLACE FOR COERCIVE PROSELYTIZING OF
NON-CHRISTIANS?
"Just as Judaism frowns on proselytizing that is coercive, or that seeks
to commit men against their will, so do I."

—ASSOCIATED PRESS, AUGUST 21, 1981

WHAT WAS YOUR OPINION OF A PLAN BY SOUTHERN BAPTISTS
TO SEND THOUSANDS OF EVANGELISTS TO CHICAGO TO TRY
TO CONVERT JEWS, HINDUS, AND MUSLIMS?
"I'm a Southern Baptist, and I normally defend my denomination.
I'm loyal to it. I believe in them. They have some of the finest people
in the world in our denomination. But I have never targeted
Muslims. I have never targeted Jews. I believe that we should declare
the fact that God loves you, God's willing to forgive you, God can
change you, and Christ and his kingdom is open to anybody who
repents and by faith receives him as Lord and Savior."

— THE VIRGINIAN-PILOT (NORFOLK), JANUARY 15, 2000

WHAT ARE YOUR THOUGHTS ABOUT ISLAM?
"There are things about Islam that appeal to people. Strict rules.
People want discipline and some authority. Still, I think Islam also is

divided, just as much as Christianity." *(On Islam's spread as one of the twentieth century's major trends)*

— *THE HERALD* (ROCK HILL, SC), JANUARY 1, 2000

CHRISTIANS AND MUSLIMS HAVE DIVERGENT VIEWS ON MANY THINGS, BUT WHAT DO BOTH RELIGIONS HAVE IN COMMON?
"Christians and Muslims admittedly disagree at certain points in their beliefs. But we can agree that God wants us to have compassion on those who are suffering and to do what we can to help."

— *THE BOSTON HERALD*, SEPTEMBER 27, 1999

WHAT IS BEHIND PEOPLE'S ATTRACTION TO CULTS?
"Cult activity is worldwide. . . . Cults are made up of people who are fanatically following a leader who leads them astray. I believe that in back of it all is the devil, who has his plans and counterfeits of Jesus Christ."

—COMMENTING ON THE HEAVEN'S GATE CULT—A GROUP OF 39 PEOPLE IN CALIFORNIA WHO COMMITTED SUICIDE BECAUSE THEY BELIEVED ALIENS WOULD RETRIEVE THEM FROM EARTH. *FORT WORTH STAR-TELEGRAM* (TEXAS), APRIL 2, 1997

HAVE YOU EVER TARGETED JEWS FOR CONVERSION?
"I have never taken part in organizations or projects that especially targeted Jews. I preach the gospel to any and all who come to our meetings."

— *THE CHARLOTTE OBSERVER* (NORTH CAROLINA), JUNE 21, 1996

WHAT DO YOU SAY TO JEWS WHO ARE CONCERNED ABOUT YOUR TRYING TO CONVERT THEM?
"There are many passages in the Bible—Old Testament and New Testament—that indicate that the Jewish people are in a special category of God's chosen people. I'm certainly not going to beg them or

coerce them or target them. I have to leave it to the spirit of God and their own decision and choice."

— *THE NEW YORK TIMES*, SEPTEMBER 16, 1991

YOU APOLOGIZED PUBLICLY FOR SOME ANTI-JEWISH
STATEMENTS YOU MADE TO PRESIDENT RICHARD NIXON IN
THE 1970S. YOU'VE ALSO NOTED THE RISE OF ANTI-SEMITISM
IN EUROPE AND SAID THAT IT AMOUNTS TO BIGOTRY AND IS A
SIN. WHAT WERE YOUR COMMENTS?

"I cannot imagine what caused me to make those comments, which I totally repudiate. Whatever the reason, I was wrong for not disagreeing with the president, and I sincerely apologize to anyone I offended. I don't ever recall having those feelings about any group, especially the Jews, and I certainly do not have them now. My remarks did not reflect my love for the Jewish people. I humbly ask the Jewish community to reflect on my actions on behalf of Jews over the years that contradict my words in the Oval Office that day. . . . Racial prejudice, anti-Semitism or hatred of anyone with different beliefs has no place in the human mind or heart."

— EXCERPTS OF A WRITTEN LETTER TO THE NEWS MEDIA.
COX NEWS SERVICE. JUNE 21. 2002

On OUR RELATIONSHIP
WITH GOD

CAN WE KNOW GOD'S PLAN FOR US?

"You never know when your hour is coming, when God is going to say, 'That's it.' Unless we turn to God, unless we thank him for all these bountiful things we have . . . judgment is coming."

— *MORNING STAR* (WILMINGTON, NC), NOVEMBER 7, 2000

HOW DOES OUR RELATIONSHIP TO GOD AFFECT OUR HEALTH?

"God has a prescription that will never fail."

— *THE FLORIDA TIMES-UNION* (JACKSONVILLE), NOVEMBER 5, 2000

HOW DOES GOD HELP YOU PREPARE FOR SERMONS?

"I come here with a sense of fear and trembling of my own inadequacy and my own lack of strength. But in our weakness there's a strength that God gives, and so I'm totally dependent on the Holy Spirit to help me."

— BEFORE A FOUR-DAY CRUSADE AT AGE EIGHTY-TWO,
KNOXVILLE NEWS-SENTINEL (TENNESSEE), NOVEMBER 1, 2000

WHAT DOES THE STORY OF NOAH'S ARK TEACH US?

"God means business. He's pronounced judgment on us if we don't repent of our sins."

— *THE TENNESSEAN*, JUNE 5, 2000

HOW CAN GOD HELP US LIVE BETTER LIVES?

"The love of God in an individual's heart can overcome all of our baser instincts and selfish motives."

—*THE COMMERCIAL APPEAL* (MEMPHIS, TN), JUNE 4, 2000

HOW DID GOD VIEW THE MILLENNIUM?

"I don't think that God looks on the millennium as we do. That's our term. God is from everlasting to everlasting." *(When asked about how God viewed the year 2000)*

—*SATURDAY EVENING POST*, NOVEMBER 1, 1999

DOES GOING TO CHURCH MEAN THAT YOU HAVE A RELATIONSHIP WITH GOD?

"You can be a member of every church in town and that doesn't mean you know God."

—*CALGARY HERALD* (ALBERTA, CANADA), OCTOBER 23, 1999

CAN YOU PROVE SCIENTIFICALLY THAT GOD EXISTS?

"No, I don't believe the existence of God can be proven by science. You can't put God to the test."

—*THE OTTAWA SUN*, JUNE 26, 1998

SOME PEOPLE THINK THEY CAN HIDE FROM GOD, THAT HE DOESN'T NOTICE THEIR SINS. WHAT DO YOU SAY TO THESE PEOPLE?

"Adam and Eve hid in the trees of the garden . . . but you can't hide from God. Don't try to run from God, run toward God."

—*THE LEDGER* (LAKELAND, FLORIDA), OCTOBER 25, 1998, DURING A TAMPA CRUSADE

DOES GOD EVER CHANGE?

"God has a plan for you and your life if you put your trust and your faith in Him. God never changes. God loves you."

—*ORLANDO SENTINEL* (FLORIDA), OCTOBER 23, 1998

"There are some things that never change. God has not changed. He's absolutely holy, and to get to heaven you have to be holy."

— *LEXINGTON HERALD LEADER* (KENTUCKY), JUNE 22, 2001

WHAT DOES GOD EXPECT OF US?

"If you fail to use each day's deposits, you cannot have overdrafts. Your only choice is to use it or lose it. The Lord expects us to use what we have whether money, time or talent."

—COMMENCEMENT ADDRESS AT PALM BEACH ATLANTIC COLLEGE,

QUOTED IN THE *SUN-SENTINEL* (FORT LAUDERDALE, FL), APRIL 27, 1997

WHAT DO YOU SAY TO PEOPLE WHO SAY THAT GOD HASN'T ANSWERED THEIR PRAYERS?

"I believe that God listens to every prayer. I think every single prayer is answered. God may say, 'No.' He may say, 'Yes, I am going to do what you're asking,' or He may say, 'It's not good for you to have this.' And He knows the end from the beginning. He knows the end of my life. He knows everything that's going to happen and everything that has happened."

—CNN's *LARRY KING LIVE*, JANUARY 21, 1997

WHY CAN'T WE DECIPHER GOD'S PLAN? WHY CAN'T WE PUT HIS MOTIVES UNDER A MICROSCOPE?

"Why is there so much disease, poverty, war, hate, racism, loneliness, boredom, unemployment, murder, divorce and suicide? It seems that in spite of our wealth, in spite of our affluence, in spite of our education—something is wrong . . . We ask ourselves, 'Who is this God that loves us? Why does a God of love allow all of this?' You can't put God in a test tube, you can't put His picture up on a screen. But that doesn't mean that He's not real. He is real, and He loves you."

—PR NEWSWIRE, SEPTEMBER 29, 1997

WHAT DOES THE BIBLE TEACH US ABOUT GETTING ALONG WITH GOD AND EACH OTHER?

"If you read about four or five Psalms a day it makes a month, and one chapter a day of Proverbs lasts a month. Psalms teaches you how to get along with God, and Proverbs teaches you how to get along with man."

— *STAR TRIBUNE* (MINNEAPOLIS, MN), JUNE 16, 1996

IS IT VITAL TO UNDERSTAND GOD TO WORSHIP HIM?

"I'm going to ask you to come and say 'yes' to Christ. You don't understand it all, or have to. You just say, 'Lord . . . I acknowledge that I have sinned. I believe that Jesus is the only way.'"

— *ROCKY MOUNTAIN NEWS* (DENVER, CO), OCTOBER 5, 1996

YOU'VE LIKENED GOD'S POWERS TO THAT OF AN MRI MACHINE. HOW SO?

"God also has a scanner that he uses not only on your body and mind, but also your soul and spirit. He knows a lot more about you than you know yourself."

— THE CANADIAN PRESS, OCTOBER 30, 1995

WHAT HAS BEEN THE RESULT OF OMITTING GOD FROM OUR LIVES?

"In taking God and religion out of our lives, we have lost our moral and spiritual bearings."

— *CHICAGO TRIBUNE*, DECEMBER 25, 1993

IS SUFFERING A NATURAL PART OF LIFE?

"Outside of the Bible, I cannot offer true, unfailing solutions. I do not pretend to be a pop psychologist or offer pat answers. . . . We can react with bitterness and hate God, as some do, or we can accept suffering as a natural part of life and determine our response to it."

— *USA TODAY*, DECEMBER 10, 1993

IN 1992, YOU ADDRESSED A GROUP OF ABOUT ONE THOUSAND
BUSINESS AND COMMUNITY LEADERS. WHAT WAS YOUR
MESSAGE OF HOPE TO THEM?

"Our world could be heading toward Armageddon. We see all things
Jesus predicted in the Gospels taking place on the front pages of our
newspapers and on our television screens every day. I believe that in
the troubles and chaos threatening our world, there can be hope."

— PR NEWSWIRE, SEPTEMBER 22, 1992

IS THERE A REASON WHY WE HAVE NATURAL DISASTERS?

"I've seen a lot of areas where there were hurricanes, tidal waves and
wars. I've never seen as much destruction as this. . . . It's okay to ask
why. There's a reason for this and you'll find out someday what it is.
Maybe you'll find it brought your family closer together." *(Spoken
outside of Homestead, Florida, city hall in the aftermath of the devastating Hurricane Andrew)*

— ASSOCIATED PRESS, SEPTEMBER 4, 1992

DOES GOD KNOW EVERYTHING THAT WE DO?

"Remember the Watergate tapes, how they surprised everybody? I'm
sure that the president never dreamed—he was keeping that for the
diary to help him write his books when he left office—never dream-
ing what was going to happen, that they would expose the conversa-
tions that went on. . . . And in some way like that God has a recording
machine. He has a television camera right on you. But he not only
has it on your outside, he has it on your inside."

— *THE POST-STANDARD* (SYRACUSE, NY), MAY 1, 1989

WHY SHOULD WE TRUST IN GOD?

"As you know, many events in life seemingly have no answers in the face of evil. But we trust in the assurance that God has given us through St. Paul that 'all things work together for good to them that love God, to them that are called according to his purpose (Romans 8:28).'"

— SPEAKING ABOUT CHURCH OF ENGLAND ENVOY TERRY WAITE, WHO WAS CAPTURED IN LEBANON DURING HIS EFFORT TO HELP FREE HOSTAGES, UNITED PRESS INTERNATIONAL, FEBRUARY 9, 1987

WHAT ONE THING IS ALWAYS CERTAIN ABOUT GOD?

"If there's one thing that Christians can be sure of, it's that God loves us. We've broken God's laws, yet He loves us."

— *THE WASHINGTON POST*, DECEMBER 21, 1985

WHAT DID YOU SAY TO THE ATHEIST WHO DIDN'T THINK THERE IS A GOD?

"I said to him: 'Why is it that all over the world, we have never found a tribe, a people that didn't worship someone? It may be a spirit in a tree. It may be something we call God. But they worship someone.' The anthropologist agreed that it was a worldwide phenomenon that they hadn't yet figured out."

— *THE NEW YORK TIMES*, OCTOBER 13, 1985, ON A CONVERSATION HE HAD IN 1984 WITH AN ANTHROPOLOGIST IN THE SIBERIAN CITY OF NOVOSIBIRSK WHO TOLD GRAHAM THAT HE WAS AN ATHEIST

IS GOD GOING TO JUDGE OUR SINS?

"If God so loved the world, why is the world in such a mess, why are there 40 wars going on, why is there so much suffering . . . in the hospitals, why are there so many problems? I want to talk about that. . . . God is a God of judgment, who is going to judge sin. He is going to judge the world. . . . God has a taping machine; he is not only going to tape what you say and do, but what you think. Every deed is written in that book under your name, and someday it will come out on a gigantic screen for everyone to see. But there is another book, because God is a God of love. If you don't get anything else out of this crusade, I want you to hear this: God loves you and . . . has taken all of your sins so you don't have to go to the judgment."

— THE OPENING SERMON AT A TEN-DAY CRUSADE, FRIDAY NIGHT AT
ANAHEIM STADIUM IN CALIFORNIA, *LOS ANGELES TIMES*, JULY 20, 1985

YOU LIKE TO TELL THE BIBLE STORY OF THE PRODIGAL SON
WHO LEAVES HIS FATHER'S HOUSE, EXHAUSTS HIMSELF IN
SINFUL LIVING, THEN RETURNS HOME IN SHAME. IS THIS A
PARABLE FOR HOW GOD LOVES US?
"The father had been waiting day after day, hoping his son would come back. He loved his son. . . . When he came, he didn't judge him, he didn't condemn him, he just loved him."

— *ORANGE COUNTY REGISTER* (CALIFORNIA), MAY 10, 2003

On SEEKING GOD

SPIRITUALLY, WHAT IS IT THAT PEOPLE SEEK BUT MAY NOT
UNDERSTAND OR BELIEVE?
"All our troubles come from the fact that man's heart is not right. All
over the world there is a thirst for something . . . people don't know
what it is they are thirsting for. They are thirsting for God." *(Speaking
at the Georgetown Baptist Church)*

— *THE WASHINGTON POST,* DECEMBER 8, 1980

WHAT WILL HAPPEN TO THOSE PEOPLE WHO ARE NOT
PREPARED FOR THE SECOND COMING OF JESUS?
"Someday Jesus Christ is coming back. That is the hope of believers. The Word of God says it will come as a devastating shock for
those who are not prepared. They will be excluded from God's
presence."

— *THE HAMILTON SPECTATOR* (ONTARIO, CANADA), MARCH 29, 1997

HOW CAN WE SURVIVE JUDGMENT DAY?
"Sometimes judgment is strange and sudden. There's an escape.
There's a way out. It's so easy. God didn't say, 'Do great things.' He
said, 'Repent and believe.'"

— *THE CHARLOTTE OBSERVER* (NORTH CAROLINA), SEPTEMBER 30, 1996

WHAT DOES IT MEAN TO "KNOW GOD"?

"When you know God, you will know how to live the Christian life. Believing in God means you put your total faith in God."

— *PLAIN DEALER* (CLEVELAND, OH), SEPTEMBER 26, 1993

FROM A CHRISTIAN POINT OF VIEW, WHAT ONE THING BINDS ALL PEOPLE TOGETHER?

"As a Christian, I believe that within every human being there is a hunger for purpose and meaning in life. Christianity teaches that only God can fill this need."

— ASSOCIATED PRESS, SEPTEMBER 6, 1985

IS IT ENOUGH TO UNDERSTAND GOD ON AN INTELLECTUAL LEVEL?

"Everyone is trying to find peace and happiness, and many times in the wrong place. There's a man in the Bible who was the richest man. The sexiest man. And the most powerful man in his generation. . . . His name was Solomon. He decided he was going to find every pleasure there is. . . . But at the end of it all he said, 'I haven't found satisfaction in any of this.' He was a man of tremendous knowledge. But you can't come to God with your mind alone."

— *CHICAGO TRIBUNE*, JUNE 25, 2001

WHAT DO YOU SAY TO PEOPLE WHO ARE SCARED TO SEEK GOD BECAUSE HE MAY IGNORE THEIR PRAYERS, OR WORSE, PUNISH THEM FOR THEIR TRANSGRESSIONS?

"God is not waiting tonight to condemn you or judge you. He is waiting to receive you in mercy and love."

— ASSOCIATED PRESS, JULY 1, 2002, FROM A SERMON IN CINCINNATI

On POLITICS

YOU HAVE SAID THAT WE SHOULD HAVE APPROACHED THE
1980S CRISIS IN IRAN IN A RELIGIOUS AND POLITICAL WAY.
WHAT DID YOU MEAN BY THAT?
"We are very ignorant of Islam and especially of the 10 percent of the
Islamic population who are Shiites—and they are the people who
control Iran. We should study them because we do not understand
their religion very much."

—ASSOCIATED PRESS, APRIL 29, 1980

AGAIN, TALKING ABOUT THE VOLATILE SITUATION IN IRAN,
WHAT ADDITIONAL ADVICE DID YOU OFFER?
"My observation is that this is a religious question. To deal with it
totally on a secular basis is not going to work."

—ASSOCIATED PRESS, APRIL 23, 1980

IS THERE A ROLE FOR RELIGION IN POLITICS?
"I think the church has to take stands on moral and social issues, but
I do not think we should be involved in partisan politics. It dilutes
the gospel."

—ASSOCIATED PRESS, JULY 30, 1981

"If I get up and talk about politics, it divides the audience. [There were times] I went too far in talking about such issues. I want to stick to the gospel."

— *PHILADELPHIA INQUIRER*, JUNE 26, 2005

WHAT ROLES DO SMALLER COUNTRIES PLAY IN THE WORLD STAGE?

"The interdependence of all nations means that every nation, whether large or small, has a vital role to play in international affairs. It also means that goodwill and understanding among peoples of different backgrounds are essential if we are to have peace and stability in our world."

—ASSOCIATED PRESS, JANUARY 8, 1981, REPORTING
ON A SPEECH GIVEN AT LUNCHEON HOSTED BY IMRE MIKLOS,
PRESIDENT OF THE HUNGARIAN CHURCH AFFAIRS OFFICE

WHAT ARE THE DANGERS OF THE CHURCH GETTING INVOLVED IN POLITICS?

"The church needs to be very wary about becoming deeply involved in political and social issues. . . . There are many very, very difficult and complex issues in this world, and we do not necessarily know the answer to them just because we are preachers or Christians."

— *RIVERFRONT TIMES* (ST. LOUIS, MO) OCTOBER 6, 1999

WHAT IS THE PUBLIC LOOKING FOR IN A POLITICIAN?

"People are looking for someone who lives in integrity. It's the way you live and how people perceive you as being different."

—RESPONSE WHEN ASKED BY SEVERAL STUDENTS ABOUT HOW TO
BALANCE THEIR CHRISTIAN FAITH WITH GOVERNMENT CAREERS, QUOTED
IN *THE STUART NEWS/PORT ST. LUCIE NEWS* (STUART, FL), OCTOBER 2, 1999

HOW DO POLITICIANS USE RELIGION FOR THEIR OWN
ENDS?

"I think some political people talk religion too much in the sense that they hope to gain favor with people who are religious."

— *PALM BEACH POST* (FLORIDA), MAY 30, 1997

YOU'VE TRIED TO BE VERY NONPARTISAN IN YOUR DEALINGS
WITH POLITICIANS. WHO DO YOU SEE AS A ROLE MODEL FOR
THIS?

"The apostle Paul skirted some political issues, when he went to places like Rome. . . . I've learned from the Scriptures . . . we have to be very diplomatic. We have to be all things to all men."

— *THE FLORIDA TIMES-UNION* (JACKSONVILLE), OCTOBER 4, 1996

HOW DO YOU AVOID TAKING SIDES IN ELECTIONS?

"I just pray that God's will be done in all these elections."

— *THE SAN FRANCISCO CHRONICLE*, OCTOBER 2, 1996

WHAT WAS YOUR FEELING WHEN THE SOVIET UNION
COLLAPSED AND THE WORLD'S MOST POWERFUL PROPONENT
OF COMMUNISM NO LONGER EXISTED?

"Communism did not win. No 'ism' is going to win. Only Christ is going to win. Someday he is going to rule the world. But tonight he wants to rule your heart."

— *THE NEW YORK TIMES*, SEPTEMBER 23, 1991

IS IT APPROPRIATE FOR THERE TO BE SPIRITUALITY AT
POLITICAL GATHERINGS?

"I'm happily surprised for clergymen to be addressing both [Republican
and Democratic] conventions. It's healthy for there to be more recog-
nition of spiritual life whenever people gather."

—AT THE NOMINATING CONVENTIONS WHICH SAW JESSE JACKSON

ADDRESS THE DEMOCRATIC PARTY AND PAT ROBERTSON ADDRESS

THE REPUBLICANS. ASSOCIATED PRESS. AUGUST 12. 1988

IS VOTING MORE THAN A CIVIC RESPONSIBILITY?

"It will be an interesting election year. The whole world is going to
be affected by who is elected. It's our civic responsibility, and religious
responsibility to get out and vote—whomever we vote for."

—PR NEWSWIRE. JULY 29. 1988

ARE EVANGELICAL CHRISTIANS POLITICALLY TYPECAST?

"People do get the impression that if you're an evangelical Christian,
you're a conservative Republican. I do feel that that idea should be
dissipated."

—*LOS ANGELES TIMES*. JULY 23. 1988

WHAT LESSON HAVE YOU LEARNED ABOUT STICKING TO THE
GOSPEL INSTEAD OF TALKING POLITICS?

"I have learned that if I stick to the gospel I do better than if I say
anything political."

—UNITED PRESS INTERNATIONAL. SEPTEMBER 12. 1984

WAS THE WAR IN IRAQ (THE SECOND GULF WAR) JUSTIFIED?
"I can't answer that at this point. It's too political right now and I'm trying to, hopefully, reach people of all persuasions with the Gospel in my job as a presenter of the Gospel of Christ."

—*LOS ANGELES TIMES*, NOVEMBER 17, 2004

YOU DECLINED TO DISCUSS POLITICS AT YOUR NEW YORK CRUSADES BECAUSE IT WOULD DETRACT FROM YOUR MAIN MESSAGE OF SALVATION THROUGH CHRIST. HOW SO?
"There were many times [in the past] where I went too far in talking about those issues. I think this time, I want to stick only to the Gospel."

—ASSOCIATED PRESS, JUNE 21, 2005

HOW HAVE YOU CHANGED YOUR VIEWS ON TAKING SIDES IN POLITICS?
"In earlier years, in the '50s and the '60s, I did take sides in some things, even in politics to an extent. I didn't mean to, but I did. But I don't do that anymore."

—*USA TODAY*, MAY 16, 2005

THE BILLY GRAHAM EVANGELISTIC ASSOCIATION FACT SHEET

Founded: 1950 by Billy Graham

PROGRAMS: The following are ministries of the Billy Graham Evangelistic Association:

Billy Graham Crusades—Billy Graham has preached the gospel to more than 210 million people in live audiences at hundreds of crusades, missions, and evangelistic rallies. His final crusade was held in New York City June 24–26, 2005, where 242,000 people attended the event. Graham developed the early use of television specials in the 1950s, which today are broadcast in the United States and Canada, reaching an average of two million households per telecast.

Franklin Graham Festivals—Since 1989, Franklin Graham has preached at more than one hundred evangelistic festivals in thirty-three states and twenty other countries. The BGEA appointed Franklin Graham CEO in 2000 and president of the organization in 2001. He has served as first vice-chairman of the BGEA since 1995. Franklin also serves as president of Samaritan's Purse, an international relief organization based in Boone, North Carolina.

My Hope—Through this movement for relationship evangelism, churches and Christian families are encouraged, trained, and mobilized to open their homes to friends and neighbors, to share the gospel using television broadcasts produced by the BGEA in local languages.

Decision **Magazine**—The official monthly publication of the BGEA, founded in 1960, has a circulation of more than six-hundred-thousand—making it one of the largest religious periodicals in the world.

Billy Graham Training Center at The Cove—This retreat center opened in 1991 to offer multi-day seminars on a variety of Christian subjects. It also offers year-round retreats.

Schools of Evangelism—These schools are training events designed to help pastors and Christian leaders to more effectively reach out to their local communities. More than 111,500 church leaders have participated in the schools in North America since their inception in 1967.

Grason—The resource ministry of the BGEA provides individuals and organizations with books, movies, music, and other material for training and growth in the Christian faith. Grason publishes original literature and other resources for distribution, including millions of copies of Billy Graham's books translated into thirty-eight languages. Grason also oversees the BGEA ministry previously known as World Wide Pictures. Beginning with *Mr. Texas*, in 1951, Billy Graham evangelistic films have been interpreted into thirty-eight languages and viewed by more than 250 million people in theaters, in churches, in prisons, and on television. The BGEA has produced and distributed more than 125 productions—from fifteen-minute television programs to 25 feature-length films.

ELECTRONIC OUTREACH:

Radio Programs—The weekly *Hour of Decision* radio program, begun in 1950, is broadcast on weekends to virtually every part of the United States and most areas of Canada. Other countries around the world receive the broadcast via short wave and medium wave radio in one of three different languages.

Telecasts—Television broadcasts of select Billy Graham Crusades and Franklin Graham Festivals air across North America during prime time. An average of 150 stations—nearly all of which are network affiliates—across the United States and Canada have carried the telecasts in prime time five to seven times annually.

Satellite Broadcasts—The BGEA's use of broadcast media was first done in 1995 through Global Mission. This conference in Puerto Rico was the largest evangelistic outreach in the history of the church. The event was transmitted via satellite to a total of ten million people at three thousand locations in 185 countries and territories.

Billy Graham Response Center—The Response Center opened in June 1998 to provide information and service to people with questions regarding the Billy Graham Evangelistic Association. The Response Center also handles calls from those needing salvation or spiritual encouragement and also serves calls for Samaritan's Purse. During 2005, the center handled more than 39,000 e-mails and 670,000 calls from individuals. The Response Center operates twenty-four hours a day, seven days a week.

Christian Guidance—The Christian Guidance department handles letters, telecast follow-up forms, phone calls, and e-mail from tens of thousands of people annually—many of whom are in desperate circumstances, experiencing many types of problems. In 2005 Christian Guidance staff responded to some 150,000 inquiries.

TV/Telephone Ministry—The TV/Telephone Ministry in conjunction with the Billy Graham event telecasts began nationwide in March 1981 and has since served more than one million people. From the privacy of their homes, people can call a telephone number on their screen to receive spiritual help and guidance.

Internet (www.BillyGraham.org)—The BGEA Internet outreach includes all of the organization's ministries and event information online. In 2005, the BGEA Web sites logged more than 7.5 million visits.

OFFICES:

The BGEA international headquarters is located on the Billy Graham Parkway in Charlotte, North Carolina. The organization also has offices in Canada, Australia, Great Britain, and Germany.

SOURCE: BILLY GRAHAM EVANGELISTIC ASSOCIATION

On POVERTY

THE DEVELOPING NATIONS ARE SADDLED WITH ENORMOUS
DEBT TO THE DEVELOPED WORLD. WHAT SHOULD BE DONE
ABOUT IT?

"Tragically, during just these next 100 days, over 2 million infants
and children in less developed countries will not live to see the
beginning of the year 2000 because of malnutrition and prevent-
able disease. . . . Most of these poor nations are saddled with enormous economic debts, debts they have no hope of ever repaying
but which nevertheless condemn them to an endless cycle of
poverty. . . . If I were a parent in a poor, debt-riddled nation,
cradling my dying child in my arms, my heart would be broken. . . .
I would cry out for a solution—that the world leaders work
together to solve this problem."

—PR NEWSWIRE, SEPTEMBER 23, 1999

FROM A CHRISTIAN POINT OF VIEW, CAN YOU JUSTIFY
SPENDING MONEY ON ARMS WHEN THAT MONEY COULD BE
SPENT ELSEWHERE TO FEED PEOPLE?

"We're spending billions and billions on bombs that will never be
used, and yet millions of people are on the verge of starvation or are
actually starving. We cannot justify that from a Christian point of
view . . . but we are not living in a Christian world—and I suppose

we have to accept the world as it is and work toward the elimination of all these arms that are draining the world of its energy and its strength and its wealth."

—PR NEWSWIRE, OCTOBER 24, 1988

On PRAYER

CAN PRAYER CHANGE THE COURSE OF HISTORY?

"From one end of the Bible to the other, we find the record of people whose prayers have been answered, people who turned the tide of history by prayer, men and women who prayed fervently and whom God answered."

—*PEMBROKE OBSERVER* (ONTARIO, CANADA), NOVEMBER 22, 2003

WHAT IS THE GREATEST FORM OF PRAYER?

"I believe that the greatest form of prayer is praise to God. We are to praise Him, because He is the mighty power back of this vast universe. Even Hubble hasn't found yet the end of this universe, and we don't know that it has any end. But back of all of that is a supernatural being that we call God. And if I know God personally, as I believe I do, that is so overwhelming I—there's no way to conceive it, no way for me to think about it, it's so beyond me. So that's the reason I have to come by faith and believe it."

—CNN's *LARRY KING LIVE*, MAY 29, 2005

On PRESIDENTS AND POLITICIANS

RONALD REAGAN

YOU AND RONALD REAGAN HAD BEEN FRIENDS FOR MANY
YEARS BEFORE HE WAS ELECTED PRESIDENT. HOW WAS YOUR
RELATIONSHIP WITH HIM DIFFERENT THAN WITH OTHER
PRESIDENTS?

"He doesn't talk politics to a person like me. He's different from other
politicians in that regard."

—UNITED PRESS INTERNATIONAL, DECEMBER 19, 1980

AND WHAT ABOUT NANCY REAGAN IN PARTICULAR?

"I think that Nancy has been really mistreated in some ways in the
press—or misunderstood. Some of them said she was cold and hard.
I found her one of the warmest, sweetest, and most interested women
I have ever known as a First Lady."

—NBC'S *TODAY*, MARCH 5, 1998

WHAT WAS YOUR OPINION OF THE REAGANS' MARRIAGE?

"The love between Ronald and Nancy Reagan was an example to the
nation."

—ASSOCIATED PRESS, JUNE 5, 2004, UPON THE DEATH OF RONALD REAGAN

WITH RONALD REAGAN, MANY AMERICANS SOUGHT A CHANGE. WHERE DID HE GET HIS STRENGTH?

"He will be a deeper and more able president than the press ever gives credit for. He won't be rigid. He will appoint and have his strength through leadership."

—UNITED PRESS INTERNATIONAL, NOVEMBER 12, 1980

HOW WOULD YOU DESCRIBE YOUR DINNER AT THE WHITE HOUSE WITH RONALD REAGAN?

"We arrived at the White House about 5 p.m. and talked 'til 10. The four of us had dinner. . . . We didn't mention politics once. . . . I get the feeling the country is in capable hands. Ronald Reagan runs it but, like Ike, he lets others handle the details, which gives him time to think of bigger things."

—ASSOCIATED PRESS, JULY 22, 1981

THERE WERE THOSE WHO CRITICIZED PRESIDENT REAGAN, SAYING HE WAS NOT RELIGIOUS BECAUSE HE DID NOT GO TO CHURCH VERY OFTEN. WHAT WAS YOUR OPINION OF THIS BELIEF?

"By your fruits shall you know them, not by their church attendance. In his life, we have seen that he bears these fruits. He seems to be at peace with himself."

— *THE WASHINGTON POST*, APRIL 16, 1984

WAS PRESIDENT REAGAN SPIRITUAL?

"He is one of the cleanest, most moral and spiritual men I know. In the scores of times we were together, he has always wanted to talk about spiritual things."

— *VENTURA COUNTY STAR* (CALIFORNIA), FEBRUARY 4, 2001, ON REAGAN'S NINETIETH BIRTHDAY

HOW DID YOU DESCRIBE PRESIDENT REAGAN UPON HIS DEATH?

"If ever we have known a child of light, it was Ronald Reagan. He was aglow with it. He had no dark side, no scary hidden agenda. What you saw was what you got, and what you saw was that sure sign of inner light, the twinkle in the eye."

— *THE NEW YORK TIMES*, JUNE 12, 2004, UPON REAGAN'S DEATH

RICHARD NIXON

EVEN AFTER HE RESIGNED THE PRESIDENCY IN DISGRACE, DID RICHARD NIXON HAVE WISDOM TO OFFER US?

"Mr. Nixon's advice should be sought in this day of problems and dilemmas of what to do. He has a greater grasp on foreign affairs than any other living American."

— UNITED PRESS INTERNATIONAL, NOVEMBER 20, 1981

DID YOU RESPECT PRESIDENT NIXON DESPITE WHAT HE DID IN OFFICE?

"Yes, I respect him. Because each man has his failures, and none of us are perfect. And Jesus said, 'He that is without sin among you, let him cast the first stone.' And so I forgive him. And I love his children. I saw Tricia the night before last—they're such a wonderful family."

— NBC'S *TODAY*, MARCH 5, 1998

SOME PEOPLE SAID YOU GOT TOO CLOSE TO RICHARD NIXON AND IT HURT YOUR REPUTATION AS ONE WHO DOESN'T TAKE SIDES IN POLITICS. WHAT HAPPENED?

"I became too close to a president [Nixon] and got identified with him and his policies. I learned my lesson and pulled completely away."

— *TELEGRAPH HERALD* (DUBUQUE, IA), MAY 30, 1999

WERE YOU SURPRISED BY THE COARSE LANGUAGE THAT YOU
HEARD IN THE NIXON TAPES?
"What comes through in these [Oval Office] tapes is not the man I
have known for many years. . . . He is my friend. . . . I have no inten-
tion of forsaking him now."

—AFTER PORTIONS OF THE TAPES WERE MADE PUBLIC IN 1974,
CITED BY *PITTSBURGH POST-GAZETTE* (PENNSYLVANIA), MAY 29, 1999

HOW DID IT MAKE YOU FEEL WHEN YOU HEARD THE TAPES?
"The thing that surprised and shook me most was the vulgar language he used. Never, in all the times I was with him, did he use language even close to that. I felt physically sick and went into the
seclusion of my study at the back of the house."

—ASSOCIATED PRESS, APRIL 26, 1997

WAS PRESIDENT NIXON MISUNDERSTOOD BY MOST
AMERICANS?
"I think he was one of the most misunderstood men, and I think he
was one of the greatest men of the century. I think people never saw
the gentle and the human and the gracious and the thoughtful side
of Richard Nixon."

—ABC'S *NIGHTLINE*, APRIL 22, 1994

WHAT DID YOU CONVEY TO THOSE PRESENT AT PATRICIA
NIXON'S FUNERAL ABOUT THE FORMER FIRST LADY?
"Few women in public life have suffered as she has suffered and done
it with such grace. In all the years I knew her, I never heard her say
anything unkind about anyone."

—*LOS ANGELES TIMES*, JUNE 27, 1993,

YOU WERE SOMEWHAT SURPRISED AT ALL THE ATTENTION THAT
WATERGATE RECEIVED IN THE MEDIA. YOU COMPARED
RICHARD NIXON TO SEVERAL BIBLICAL FIGURES. HOW SO?
"Look at David. He had to run and hide. And then he committed a
murder and he committed adultery, which was abhorrent to God. But
God forgave David and David is considered one of the greatest kings
that ever lived in the history of Judaism. . . . If we would have had the
cameras on David in those days, they might have rebelled against
him. We would have had black headlines. . . . I have read a lot about
Watergate, but I still don't understand it. I don't understand why it
became such a big thing, and neither do the people around the
world."

— *LOS ANGELES TIMES*, JULY 19, 1990

JOHN F. KENNEDY
WHAT WERE YOUR IMPRESSIONS OF JOHN F. KENNEDY AND
FIRST LADY JACKIE?
"They were one of the nicest young couples I have ever met. But
when they got on that plane a few months ago they never dreamed
that that would be their last day together."

— *CALGARY SUN* (ALBERTA, CANADA), OCTOBER 15, 1999

WAS KENNEDY'S WIN A VICTORY FOR RELIGION IN AMERICA?
"Mr. Kennedy's victory had proved there was not as much religious
prejudice as many had feared, and probably had reduced forever the
importance of the religious issue in American elections."

— CITING A JANUARY 17, 1961 *NEW YORK TIMES*

ARTICLE, *THE NEW YORK TIMES*, OCTOBER 31, 1992

YOU HAVE A GREAT MYSTERY ABOUT SOMETHING PRESIDENT
KENNEDY DID NOT SAY TO YOU. WHAT WAS THAT STORY ABOUT?
"I had spoken at a breakfast and John Kennedy was sitting beside me.
And he whispered to me, he said, 'Will you ride back to the White
House with me?' And I said, 'You know, Mr. President,' I said, 'I'm
sick.' I said, 'I have a fever and I don't think I ought to ride in the car
with you and go to the White House. Let me come over some other
time.' And he smiled and he said, 'OK.' And I have often wondered
what did he want to talk about? And I never got that opportunity
because he died a few months later. And that, to me, is a mystery that
I would like cleared up when I get to heaven."

— *FLORIDA TODAY* (BREVARD COUNTY, FLORIDA), JULY 2, 2005,

CITING AN NBC TELEVISION INTERVIEW

GEORGE W. BUSH
DO YOU EVER ENDORSE CANDIDATES?
"I don't endorse candidates. But I've come as close to it, I guess, now
as any time in my life because I think it's extremely important. I
believe in the integrity of this man." *(About George W. Bush, at a
Jacksonville, Florida, crusade)*

— *THE STATE* (COLUMBIA, SC), JANUARY 5, 2001

WHAT WAS YOUR OPINION OF GEORGE W. BUSH BEFORE AND
DURING THE 2000 ELECTION CAMPAIGN?
"We believe that there's going to be a tremendous victory and change
by Tuesday night in the direction of the country, putting it in good
hands. I believe in the integrity of this man. . . . And if they, by God's
will, win, I'm going to do everything in my power to help them make
it a successful presidency."

— *HOUSTON CHRONICLE*, NOVEMBER 6, 2000;

THE BOSTON GLOBE, NOVEMBER 6, 2000

DO YOU CONSIDER GEORGE W. BUSH A FRIEND?

"I'm very thankful for the privilege of calling him [George Bush] friend, and his wife."

—KNIGHT RIDDER WASHINGTON BUREAU, NOVEMBER 6, 2000

DO PEOPLE HAVE THE WRONG IMPRESSION ABOUT GEORGE BUSH?

"They think he's a man of little substance, but that's not true. I think that he's a man of tremendous moral character to begin with, and what they have written about his earlier years could be true of nearly all of us."

—*THE NEW YORK TIMES*, JANUARY 23, 2000

WHAT WAS YOUR REACTION WHEN YOU HEARD THAT THEN TEXAS GOVERNOR GEORGE W. BUSH NAMED JESUS CHRIST AS THE PHILOSOPHER OR THINKER WHO'D HAD THE MOST IMPACT ON HIS LIFE?

"It was a wonderful answer. I mean, to millions of young people, especially in the United States, Jesus Christ is the greatest man in this—in the history of the world. And to me, he's the greatest person in the history of mankind and the universe. We can't prove it, I can't put it in a test tube or in an astronomical formula, but by faith I believe it because the Bible teaches it."

—ASSOCIATED PRESS, JANUARY 2, 2000

WHAT SORTS OF RELIGIOUS THINGS DID GEORGE BUSH WANT TO KNOW WHEN HE TALKED WITH YOU PRIVATELY?

"He wanted to know more about what it means to be a Christian, to be a moral leader, and he always impressed me as a man that had his goal of being something more than just the son of George Bush."

—*THE WICHITA EAGLE*, OCTOBER 26, 2000

ARE YOU IMPRESSED BY GEORGE BUSH'S UP-FRONT ATTITUDE
ABOUT ACCEPTING CHRIST?
"He says straight out that he has received Christ as his Savior, that
he's a born-again believer and that he reads the bible daily. Bush has
the highest moral standards of almost anybody I have known."

—PR NEWSWIRE, MAY 21, 1990, CITING *TIME* MAGAZINE

WHAT WERE YOUR FEELINGS WHEN PRESIDENT GEORGE W.
BUSH SALUTED THE TROOPS ABOARD THE USS *ABRAHAM
LINCOLN* AFTER TEN MONTHS AT SEA?
"I try to stay out of politics but I thought that was great. It gave us a
sense of leadership at a time of war."

—ASSOCIATED PRESS, MAY 10, 2003

HOW DO YOU THINK PRESIDENT BUSH HANDLED THE
AFTERMATH OF 9/11?
"I think he has stepped up to the plate. I've known him since he was
a teenager, and I think he has handled it [in a] far superior [way] than
I had thought he would be able to."

—*MODESTO BEE*, OCTOBER 7, 2001

PRESIDENT BUSH WAS CRITICIZED BY SOME FOR LANDING ON
AN AIRCRAFT CARRIER, PROCLAIMING "MISSION
ACCOMPLISHED" FOR THE IRAQ WAR. WHAT WAS YOUR
REACTION TO HIS FLIGHT?
"I thought it was a courageous thing that he did. It's like the world's
largest slingshot."

—*TULSA WORLD* (OKLAHOMA), JUNE 11, 2003

WHAT WAS THE PRAYER YOU OFFERED TO THE COUNTRY UPON
GEORGE W. BUSH'S RE-ELECTION TO A SECOND TERM AS
PRESIDENT?

"Their next four years are hidden from us, but they are not hidden from
you. You know the challenges and opportunities they will face. Give
them a clear mind, a warm heart, calmness in the midst of turmoil,
reassurance in times of discouragement and your presence always."

—ASSOCIATED PRESS, JANUARY 21, 2005

GEORGE H. W. BUSH

THE NIGHT BEFORE THE FIRST GULF WAR STARTED, YOU WERE
WITH GEORGE H. W. BUSH AND HIS WIFE AT THE WHITE HOUSE.
DID THE PRESIDENT ASK YOUR ADVICE ABOUT INVADING IRAQ?

"He didn't ask my opinion or my advice, and the next day I spoke at
a service for troops and military leaders."

—*ST. PETERSBURG TIMES* (FLORIDA), MAY 22, 1991

LYNDON B. JOHNSON

WHAT WAS YOUR RELATIONSHIP TO PRESIDENT JOHNSON?

"I tried to be a spiritual counselor to Lyndon Johnson, but I was not
his confessor."

—*U.S. NEWS & WORLD REPORT*, MAY 5, 1997, CITING GRAHAM'S BOOK *JUST AS I AM*

DID IT BOTHER YOU WHEN PRESIDENT JOHNSON USED FOUL
LANGUAGE?

"The language he used with other people he used in front of me, and
he'd say, 'Excuse me, Reverend.' Or he'd say, 'Excuse me, Billy.' . . . I
care about it if they use the name of God, or if they say Jesus Christ.
Why don't they say Mohamed or something else? Or Buddha? But

it's always Jesus Christ. Why is that? I don't know. You know, it grates on me, and he knew that."

—ABC NEWS *PRIMETIME LIVE*, DECEMBER 17, 1992

WHAT DID YOU SAY ABOUT PRESIDENT JOHNSON UPON HIS DEATH?
"No one could ever understand Lyndon Johnson unless they understood the land and the people from which he came." *(Speaking at President Johnson's funeral)*

—*ST. PETERSBURG TIMES* (FLORIDA), JUNE 8, 2003

BILL CLINTON
WHAT'S YOUR RELATIONSHIP WITH BILL CLINTON?
"What I have to say, for example, to the president [Bill Clinton], I wouldn't say publicly, but I have known him since he was about 12 or 14 years of age and we've been friends all these years."

—*OTTAWA CITIZEN*, JUNE 24, 1998

AGAIN, THINKING OF BILL CLINTON AND OTHER PRESIDENTS, IS THERE A DANGER THAT A POLITICIAN'S PRIVATE INDISCRETIONS CAN CARRY OVER INTO HIS PUBLIC LIFE?
"We must not be tempted to divorce character from leadership. That would be tragic."

—*THE WEEKEND AUSTRALIAN*, MARCH 21, 1998

WHAT DID YOU TELL PRESIDENT CLINTON AFTER HE VETOED LEGISLATION CRIMINALIZING PARTIAL-BIRTH ABORTIONS?
"I think the president was wrong in vetoing it. I had the opportunity of telling him that in person."

—*THE WASHINGTON TIMES*, MAY 2, 1996

YOU'VE SAID THAT PRESIDENT CLINTON SHOULD FULFILL HIS
GRANDMOTHER'S PROPHECY AND BECOME AN EVANGELIST
MINISTER WHEN HE LEAVES THE WHITE HOUSE. WHAT MADE
YOU SAY THAT?

"He believes the Bible. He believes in God. He believes in Christ. He
believes that he has been born again. He's got all the gifts an evangelist should have."

— *THE BALTIMORE SUN*, OCTOBER 14, 1996

WHEN THE PRESS WAS FASCINATED BY PRESIDENT CLINTON'S
SEXUAL MISCONDUCT, YOU SUGGESTED THAT THEY LOOK
ELSEWHERE FOR STORIES. WHAT DID YOU SAY TO THEM?

"We're in a worldwide mess right now [Bosnia, Rwanda and the
nuclear threat in North Korea]. We need to emphasize that, rather
than some mistake the president may make or some failure in character, because none of us is perfect."

— *SOUTH BEND TRIBUNE* (INDIANA), APRIL 17, 1994, CITING A SPEECH TO
THE AMERICAN SOCIETY OF NEWSPAPER EDITORS IN WASHINGTON, DC

YOU HAVE OFFERED PRAYERS AT MANY PRESIDENTIAL
INAUGURATIONS, BUT WERE ASKED BY SOME NOT TO
PARTICIPATE IN BILL CLINTON'S SWEARING IN BECAUSE OF
HIS STANCE ON ABORTION. WHY DID YOU REJECT THOSE
CALLS TO STAY AWAY?

"I'm praying for the President, not for a party or a platform. We're
told to pray for the people in authority. Jacob prayed for Pharaoh and
Daniel prayed for Nebuchadnezzar."

— *THE NEW YORK TIMES*, JANUARY 16, 1993

GERALD FORD

YOU REASSURED PRESIDENT GERALD FORD THAT PARDONING RICHARD NIXON WOULD BE THE PROPER THING TO DO. WHAT THOUGHTS DID YOU HAVE ABOUT FORD AND HIS PRESIDENCY?

"He was always to me a man of tremendous integrity and held the highest moral values. He didn't neglect his spiritual life when he was in Washington, and I think that was one of his secrets of how he became so strong in the lives of his fellow Americans."

—ASSOCIATED PRESS, AUGUST 19, 1999

DWIGHT DAVID EISENHOWER

WAS PRESIDENT DWIGHT D. EISENHOWER A SPIRITUAL PRESIDENT?

"I think Eisenhower was. He very strongly believed that we need to turn to God—for spiritual awakening in this country. And a lot of his speeches indicate that, a lot of the things he said. I knew him before he became president. He asked me to come to Paris to see him when he was supreme commander. I flew over with my wife. We had two or three hours with him. And then he thought I could help him write speeches. So, when he was nominated, he asked me to come to Chicago and then later to Denver. And I did. I spent quite a bit of time with him. And that was one of the things that was on his heart. He wanted a spiritual awakening in this country. And I think going to church as faithfully as he did, he went to the church that I recommended to him."

—MSNBC's *HARDBALL*, JUNE 27, 2005

WHAT IS THE IMPORTANCE OF THE PRESIDENT'S ANNUAL PRAYER BREAKFAST?

"Every president since 1954 has continued the tradition of the massive annual prayer breakfast. I believe the prayer breakfast movement has played a significant role in the revival of religious interest in America."

— *THE WASHINGTON POST*, FEBRUARY 6, 1981

WHAT DID YOU SAY TO HELP HEAL THE POLITICAL RIFT AFTER THE CONTROVERSIAL 2000 PRESIDENTIAL ELECTION?

"I am encouraged that democracy has prevailed as our nation has negotiated a difficult impasse. The time has come to put aside the strong rhetoric that can only divide us and unite for the greater good as 'one nation under God.' He alone can bring us together."

— *THE TENNESSEAN*, DECEMBER 16, 2000

WHAT DO YOU SAY TO PEOPLE WHO ARE DISENFRANCHISED BY OUR POLITICAL SYSTEM AND DON'T VOTE?

"Bad politicians are elected by good people who don't vote."

— *THE TIMES* (SHREVEPORT, LA), NOVEMBER 7, 2000

WHAT WORDS OF COMFORT DID YOU WRITE TO ELIZABETH DOLE WHEN SHE DROPPED HER BID AS PRESIDENTIAL CANDIDATE OF THE REPUBLICAN PARTY?

"I have always loved and admired you, and felt that you would make a great leader for our country. But since, many months ago, you put the entire process in God's hands, we must accept it as His will. . . . The Lord is preparing both you and Bob for something even more important. I am sure that is hard to believe at the moment. Please don't be discouraged."

—ASSOCIATED PRESS, OCTOBER 25, 1999

DO PRESIDENTS HAVE AN OBLIGATION TO BEHAVE BETTER THAN THE REST OF US?

"I think that a president should attempt, with God's help, to have a higher moral standard than perhaps the average man in the public has."

— *THE WASHINGTON TIMES*, MARCH 6, 1998

WHAT WAS YOUR IMPRESSION UPON MEETING BOB DOLE?

"Bob Dole is a deeply spiritual person. He has a strong religious side to him that most people don't know about."

— *THE BALTIMORE SUN*, OCTOBER 13, 1996

YOU'VE TRIED NOT TO ENDORSE CANDIDATES, BUT SOMETIMES IT'S NOT EASY TO REMAIN IMPARTIAL, IS IT?

"I don't want to get into any kind of politics—right or left or Republican or Democrat. Because I experienced that a few times in my years that you can get into trouble real fast."

— *PALM BEACH POST* (FLORIDA), OCTOBER 4, 1996

WHAT'S YOUR STANCE ON PRESIDENTIAL GOSSIP?

"I've had the privilege of knowing 10 presidents, and I've known every one of them before they ever went to the White House. They became friends. And I learned some things during those years, but I'm not going to tell any of them that are negative or bad. But I know some."

— *SEATTLE POST-INTELLIGENCER*, JUNE 24, 1995

DO YOU HAVE ANY INFLUENCE WITH U.S. PRESIDENTS?

"Always, in the back of my mind, I said this is a way to serve God, not only to influence them spiritually and religiously, but to influence the people that they influence. And second, that this is a voice that they don't hear. Very few people will tell the president about spiritual things and religious things or have prayer with him, and I felt that this was a way that God used me, and I felt I was a servant of God when I was with these people."

— THE WASHINGTON TIMES, FEBRUARY 6, 1993, CITING

AN INTERVIEW WITH DAVID FROST ON PBS

HOW DOES INTEGRITY HELP A POLITICAL LEADER?
"In a man's personal life, integrity provides confidence in the face of uncertainty. If you are to be a leader, to make a lasting and positive impact on our world you are going to have to be a man or woman with integrity."

— THE TORONTO STAR, OCTOBER 26, 1988

DID YOU HOPE THAT POLITICIANS WOULD COME TO SEE YOU
DURING YOUR WASHINGTON, DC CRUSADE?
"Political leaders sometimes need the Lord more than anybody else. I'm hoping that some will find the Lord, but I certainly would not publicize, that I would call their names or anything like that to embarrass them."

—ASSOCIATED PRESS, APRIL 24, 1986

EVEN THOUGH YOU ARE NOT A POLITICAL PERSON, YOU HAVE
SOME THOUGHTS ABOUT CHANGING THE GOVERNMENT. WHAT
ARE YOUR SUGGESTIONS FOR THE EXECUTIVE BRANCH?
"We need reform in all three branches of our government. I think the presidency itself needs to be looked at, not the man, but the whole institution. It's gotten almost too much for one man. We need a ceremonial president and we need an executive president or an executive vice president that would be more like the Europeans have. . . . I

would be in favor of something like that because I have watched these presidents and it just about kills them."

— *TULSA WORLD* (OKLAHOMA), OCTOBER 3, 2004

MANY PEOPLE ARE SURPRISED TO KNOW THAT YOU'VE NEVER PUBLICLY ENDORSED A PRESIDENTIAL CANDIDATE. WHY DO PEOPLE HAVE THIS WRONG PERCEPTION?
"Some people have thought I did, but that was because of my personal friendship with some of the presidents."

— ASSOCIATED PRESS, SEPTEMBER 10, 1980

BUT DIDN'T YOU ONCE ENDORSE A POLITICAL CANDIDATE?
"I never endorsed but one politician that I know of, and that was the governor of Texas many years ago. And I regret that, even though he got elected." *(Referring to Texas governor and close friend John B. Connolly)*

— *THE RECORD* (KITCHENER-WATERLOO, ONTARIO), JUNE 18, 2005

BOOKS ABOUT
BILLY GRAHAM

Aeseng, Nathan. *Billy Graham*. Grand Rapids, MI: Zondervan, 1993.

America's Hour of Decision. Wheaton, IL: Van Kampen, 1951.

Babbage, Stuart Barton and Ian Siggins. *Light Beneath the Cross*. New York: Doubleday, 1960.

Bishop, Mary. *Billy Graham: America's Evangelist*. New York: Grosset & Dunlap, 1978.

Brabham, Lewis F. *A New Song in the South: The Story of the Billy Graham Greenville, SC Crusade*. Grand Rapids: Zondervan, 1966.

Burnham, George. *Billy Graham: A Mission Accomplished*. Old Tappan, NJ: Fleming Revell, 1955.

————. *To the Far Corners with Billy Graham in Asia*. Old Tappan, NJ: Fleming Revell, 1956.

Burnham, George and Lee Fisher. *Billy Graham and the New York Crusade*. Grand Rapids: Zondervan, 1957.

Chapple, Arthur R. *Billy Graham*. Marshall, Morgan & Scott, 1954.

Colquhoun, Frank. *Haringay Story*. London: Hodder & Stoughton, 1955.

Cook, Charles Thomas. *The Billy Graham Story*. Wheaton, IL: Van Kampen, 1954.

————. *London Hears Billy Graham*. Grason Co., 1954.

England, Edward Oliver. *Afterwards: A Journalist Sets out to Discover What Happened to Some of Those Who Made a Decision for Christ during the Billy Graham Crusades in Britain in 1954 and 1955.* Cheltenham, England: Elim, 1957.

Ferm, Robert O. *Cooperative Evangelism: Is Billy Graham Right or Wrong?* Grand Rapids: Zondervan, 1958.

————. *Persuaded to Live: Conversion Stories from the Billy Graham Crusades.* Old Tappan, NJ: Fleming Revell, 1958.

Fey, Harold E. and Margaret Frakes, eds. *The Christian Century Reader: Representative Articles, Editorials, and Poems Selected from More than Fifty Years of the Christian Century.* Association Press, 1962.

Frady, Marshall. *Billy Graham: A Parable of American Righteousness.* Boston: Little, Brown, 1979.

Frost, Sir David. *Billy Graham: Personal Thoughts of a Public Man.* Colorado Springs, CO: Chariot, 1997.

Gillenson, Lewis W. *Billy Graham: The Man and His Message.* New York: Fawcett, 1954.

High, Stanley. *Billy Graham: The Personal Story of the Man, His Message and His Mission.* New York: McGraw, 1956.

Hutchinson, Warner and Cliff Wilson. *Let the People Rejoice.* Wellington, New Zealand: Crusader Bookroom Society, 1959.

Kilgore, James E. *Billy Graham the Preacher.* Smithtown, NY: Exposition, 1968.

Levy, Alan. *God Bless You Real Good: My Crusade with Billy Graham.* New York: Essandess, 1969.

Martin, William. *A Prophet with Honor: The Billy Graham Story.* New York: Morrow, 1991.

McLaughlin, William Gerald. *Billy Graham: Revivalist in a Secular Age.* New York: Ronald Press Co., 1960.

Meet Billy Graham: A Pictorial Record of the Evangelist, His Family and His Team. New York: Pitkin Press, 1966.

Mitchell, C. C. *Billy Graham: Saint or Sinner?* Old Tappan, NJ: Fleming Revell, 1979.

Mitchell, Curtis. *God in the Garden: The Story of the Billy Graham New York Crusade.* New York: Doubleday, 1957.

————. *Billy Graham: The Making of a Crusader.* Radnor, PA: Chilton, 1966.

Niebuhr, Reinhold. *Essays in Applied Christianity.* New York: Meridian Books, 1959.

Poling, D. *Why Billy Graham?* Grand Rapids: Zondervan, 1977.

Pollock, John C. *Billy Graham: The Authorized Biography.* 1966. Reprint, Harper New York: McGraw, 1979.

Priestley, J. B. *Thoughts in the Wilderness.* New York: Harper, 1957.

Stein, Maurice, Arthur J. Vidich, and David Manning White, eds. *Identity and Anxiety: Survival of the Person in Mass Society.* New York: Free Press, 1960.

Streiker, Lowell D. and Gerald S. Strober. *Religion and the New Majority: Billy Graham, Middle America, and the Politics of the 70s.* New York City: Association Press, 1972.

Strober, Gerald S. Graham. Boston: G. K. Hall, 1977.

————. *Billy Graham: His Life and Faith* (for juveniles). Waco, TX: Word Books, 1977.

Wellman, Sam. *Billy Graham: The Great Evangelist.* Uhrichsville, OH: Barbour, 1996.

Wirt, Sherwood Eliot. *Crusade and the Golden Gate.* New York: Harper, 1959.

————. *Billy: A Personal Look at Billy Graham, the World's Best-Loved Evangelist.* Wheaton, IL: Crossway, 1997.

On RACE

WHY DID YOU SPEAK OUT AGAINST CHURCH SEGREGATION AT
A TIME WHEN FEW CLERGY WERE DOING SO?
"I don't think there is a single social issue I haven't spoken on.
Especially on the race question. Because in the '50s, I wrote major
articles in *Life* magazine and *Reader's Digest*, saying church is the
most segregated hour of the week. I took trips with Martin Luther
King. I became friends with so many civil rights leaders."

— *ST. PAUL PIONEER PRESS* (MINNESOTA), JUNE 15, 1996

WHAT IS THE SOURCE OF MOST ETHNIC STRIFE?
"We don't yet know whether this is a conspiracy or copycat crime, but
the problem between various ethnic groups is worldwide—it is a
problem of the heart." *(Commenting on dozens of black churches that
were intentionally burned in the South)*

— *THE ATLANTA JOURNAL AND CONSTITUTION,* JUNE 13, 1996

WAS THE CHURCH LATE TO EMBRACE INTEGRATION?
"The state, the sports world and even the business field are way ahead
of the church in getting together racially. Church people should be
the first to step forward and practice what Christ taught—that there
is no difference in the sight of God." *(Speaking about a Chattanooga,*

Tennessee, crusade in 1953, when Graham personally removed ropes marking the section reserved for blacks)

— *THE CHARLOTTE OBSERVER* (NORTH CAROLINA), SEPTEMBER 24, 1996

WHY WAS RACIAL INTEGRATION OF CHURCHES SO IMPORTANT TO YOU?

"I'd like to see more openness, churches going out of their way to welcome people of another race. I don't think there's anything more wonderful than blacks and whites singing together, taking communion together."

— *THE CHARLOTTE OBSERVER* (NORTH CAROLINA), OCTOBER 10, 1995

THE RENUNCIATION OF RACISM BY THE SOUTHERN BAPTIST CONVENTION WAS A GREAT STEP FORWARD, ESPECIALLY WHEN THE PRIMARILY WHITE CONVENTION APOLOGIZED FOR PAST STANDS ON SLAVERY AND CIVIL RIGHTS AND ASKED FORGIVENESS FROM BLACK AMERICANS. WHAT WAS YOUR REACTION TO THESE PROCEEDINGS?

"I've been heartened that in this convention you have been dealing with the struggles of racism and the issue of slavery. God wants us to pull down the barriers that divide us . . . I want to say, 'Thank God.' That'll help my ministry all over the world."

— *NEWS & RECORD* (GREENSBORO, NC), JUNE 23, 1995

WHAT ARE SOME SIMPLE THINGS PEOPLE CAN DO TO BUILD RACIAL HARMONY IN THE UNITED STATES?

"We should entertain people in our homes who are of other ethnic groups. There needs to be a mixing of our ethnic backgrounds, so we can truly become one nation."

— *THE VANCOUVER SUN* (BRITISH COLUMBIA), APRIL 30, 1994

WHAT WAS YOUR REACTION TO SEEING RACIAL AND
RELIGIOUS SEGREGATION THROUGHOUT THE UNITED STATES
DURING THE '30S, '40S, AND '50S?

"I burned inwardly when once I stopped at a West Coast motel and
saw them turning away a Mexican—just because he was a Mexican.
I burned again, when on the East Coast, I saw a sign over a restaurant saying 'Gentiles Only.' Can a Christian stand aside and say, 'Let
those people suffer those indignities'? Did not Christ say, 'And as you
wish that men should do to you, do so to them?' Does the Bible not
teach, 'You shall love your neighbor as yourself'? We must enter into
their difficulties and problems, and their burdens must be our burdens, if we are to fulfill the law of Christ."

— *ORLANDO SENTINEL* (FLORIDA), NOVEMBER 7, 1992,

CITING A 1956 ARTICLE IN *LIFE* MAGAZINE

WHAT WAS YOUR REACTION TO THE RODNEY KING VERDICT
IN WHICH WHITE POLICE OFFICERS WERE ACQUITTED ON
CHARGES OF BEATING A BLACK MAN IN LOS ANGELES? THE
VERDICT SPURRED RIOTS IN LOS ANGELES AND OTHER CITIES.

"The problems we face are not only social or political in nature. They
are moral and spiritual problems which come from the selfishness
and greed of the human heart. . . . I sensed then that in some ways
little had changed since the Watts riots and that the whole area was
a powder keg just waiting for a match to be struck. Unfortunately, the
verdict in the Rodney King trial provided that match."

— *THE WASHINGTON TIMES*, MAY 3, 1992; UNITED PRESS

INTERNATIONAL, APRIL 30, 1992

WHAT WAS MARTIN LUTHER KING JR.'S ADVICE TO YOU ABOUT
PROMOTING RACE RELATIONS?

"I did not march in the streets. And that came about as a result par-
tially of a conversation I had with Martin Luther King. He said,

'Billy, I think you ought to do just what you're doing, have integrated crusades in these stadiums.' He said, 'That helps prepare the way for me in the South.' And he said, 'You keep doing that, and I'll take to the streets, but if you go to the streets, your people will desert you, and you won't have the opportunity to have these integrated crusades.' I don't think it was a mistake, because I think if I had done that, I would have lost the following that I had in the South and lost some of the influence that I had. I'm not sure."

—*THE MACNEIL/LEHRER NEWSHOUR*, APRIL 17, 1992

ARE AMERICANS FACING THE CHALLENGES OF RACISM?
"We need to face the problem. Regardless of the color of our skin, we need to love each other, and we need to bring ourselves together and realize that we are created in the image of God. I didn't ask to be born white. You didn't ask to be born black or brown or whatever color skin you have. You were made in the image of God. God created you and God has a purpose for you and He loves you—whoever you are."

—PR NEWSWIRE, SEPTEMBER 9, 1991

HAS RACIAL HARMONY ALWAYS PLAYED A PART IN YOUR MINISTRY?
"I've always been interested in the race question, and make it a part of my ministry. When I found that churches of both races were involved [in crusade efforts] it encouraged me to say yes if God gives me the strength."

—*THE FRESNO BEE* (CALIFORNIA), OCTOBER 7, 2001

HOW DO YOU VIEW A RACIALLY DIVERSE AUDIENCE?
"We need to get to know each other on a whole different level and recognize each other without knowing even what the color of the skin is, and just love each other."

—*ATLANTA INQUIRER*, OCTOBER 30, 1999

On SERMONS

WHAT DO YOU SAY TO PEOPLE WHO SAY THAT THERE'S
NOTHING NEW IN YOUR PREACHING?

"The message I'm trying to get over is very old, it's very simple, there's nothing new about it. And many times it's quoted in the press, 'He didn't say anything new.' Well, there's nothing new to say about the Gospel. . . . I'm not a great intellectual."

— *CHRISTIAN SCIENCE MONITOR*, JUNE 3, 1982

YOU'VE ALWAYS THOUGHT OF YOURSELF AS PREACHING SIMPLE
TRUTHS. CAN YOU BOIL DOWN YOUR MAIN MESSAGE TO ONE
SENTENCE?

"If you forget everything I say in this crusade, remember one thing: God loves you."

— *THE INDIANAPOLIS STAR*, JUNE 4, 1999

HOW ELSE WOULD YOU DESCRIBE YOUR BASIC MESSAGE?

"The message I preach is one of hope, that Christ offers all of us a way, and through that way we can find our future in heaven."

— NEWS CONFERENCE BEFORE A CRUSADE IN TAMPA,
COX NEWS SERVICE, OCTOBER 25, 1998

HAS YOUR PREACHING STYLE CHANGED OVER THE YEARS?
"I had a lapel microphone and I'd walk back and forth and preach as though there was no amplification. Back then I preached with much more fire and vigor. Part of that was youthfulness, part of it was intensity, part of it was conviction. And part of it was . . . part of it was ignorance. I've traveled now to 85 countries and I've become friends with people in different parts of the world and seen how they live. I think I'm definitely more tolerant than I was back then."

— *THE DALLAS MORNING NEWS*, NOVEMBER 7, 1994

WHAT IS THE MAIN MESSAGE OF ALL YOUR SERMONS?
"I try to stick to one message. The message is Christ, and him crucified. I don't see any other hope."

— *THE ATLANTA JOURNAL AND CONSTITUTION*, OCTOBER 24, 1994

PREACHING TAKES A LOT OF STAMINA. HOW DO YOU PREPARE?
"I spend quite a bit of time in bed during the day. I need all the strength I can get for the evening meeting. . . . Billy Sunday used to spend all day in bed. And I used to think, 'How lazy!' Now I understand."

— *THE NEW YORK TIMES*, OCTOBER 12, 1994

DO YOU CHANGE YOUR SERMONS BASED ON WHERE YOU ARE AT THE TIME?
"It won't be any different. I've found as I've traveled around the world that the heart of man is the same. . . . As I meet people and as I go along, I'll pick up little things that we can use. I try to make it relevant [to the area and the people]."

— *NEWSDAY* (NEW YORK), SEPTEMBER 19, 1990

HOW DO YOU KNOW THAT YOUR MESSAGE ENDURES?
"I'll be preaching some of the same sermons I preached in 1949. The Gospel hasn't changed, and people's hearts haven't changed—they're still in need of the affection the Gospel can give."

—SPEAKING PRIOR TO A CRUSADE IN SAN DIEGO,
GRAND FORKS HERALD, NOVEMBER 27, 2004

YOU'VE SAID THAT YOU'VE PREACHED THE SAME THREE OR FOUR SERMONS SINCE YOU BEGAN PREACHING. WHAT HAS CHANGED IN THEIR DELIVERY?
"My sermons are shorter than they used to be."

—RELIGION NEWS SERVICE, JUNE 24, 2005

WHY DO PEOPLE SOMETIMES MISS YOUR SIMPLE MESSAGE?
"The message is so simple that millions stumble over it. You don't have to straighten out your life first. You don't have to make yourself well before going to a doctor. You can come to Christ. You don't have to change your clothes and put on your Sunday best. The word 'believe' implies commitment and surrender."

—SERMON DURING THE COLUMBUS CRUSADE,
THE COLUMBUS DISPATCH (OHIO), SEPTEMBER 23, 1993

On SIN

HOW DO WE KNOW IF WE HAVE SINNED?
"If you have not loved God with all your heart . . . since the day you were born, you have sinned; if you have not loved your neighbor as yourself—no matter what the color of his skin—you have sinned; if you have carried hate in your heart, you have sinned."

— *THE FLORIDA TIMES-UNION* (JACKSONVILLE), OCTOBER 29, 2000

WHAT DO YOU SAY TO YOUNG PEOPLE WHO BELIEVE THEY HAVE A LOT OF TIME TO REPENT FOR THEIR SINS?
"The truth for every one of us here is that our lives could end before the sunrise tomorrow morning. Every time the clock ticks, it says, 'Now, Now, Now . . .' I tell you tonight your soul is the most important possession you have. Where your soul spends eternity is something you need to decide right now."

— *THE TENNESSEAN*, JUNE 4, 2000

ARE SINS DONE IN PRIVATE THE SAME AS SINS DONE OVERTLY?
"There is sin abroad in this land. When the mantle of darkness settles down over this city [St. Louis] at night, sin, immorality, crime and corruption take over. What happens behind closed doors, in parked

cars, in darkened taverns, in hotel rooms? It is a stench to the nostrils of the Lord."

— SERMON DURING A CRUSADE IN ST. LOUIS, CITED IN
RIVERFRONT TIMES (MISSOURI), OCTOBER 20, 1999

ARE ANY OF OUR SINS HIDDEN FROM GOD?
"Like the Watergate tapes, it [your sins] will all be there. . . . All your files can be deleted. That's what Jesus Christ was doing on that cross—loving you, taking all your sins."

— *ST. LOUIS POST-DISPATCH* (MISSOURI), OCTOBER 16, 1999

YOU'VE SAID THAT REPENTANCE MEANS A WILLINGNESS TO CHANGE THE WAY WE'VE BEEN DOING THINGS. WHAT DID YOU MEAN BY THAT?
"Repentance means being sorry enough to quit. When we repent, it means we turn around and go the opposite direction."

— *INDIANA DAILY STUDENT*, JUNE 10, 1999

WHAT DO YOU SAY TO THOSE WHO ATTEND YOUR SERMONS, HOPING TO BE ABSOLVED OF THEIR SINS?
"If you have come to me, you have made a serious mistake. I do not have the power to forgive your sins. Only God can do that through the power of Christ."

— COPLEY NEWS SERVICE, JUNE 9, 1999

DO YOU FEAR THAT PEOPLE GO TO CHURCH THINKING THAT IT AUTOMATICALLY RIDS THEM OF THEIR SINS?
"There is no doubt that we are experiencing the greatest wave of religious resurgence in American history. But one great danger, I fear, is that religion has gotten so popular that it has become the social thing

to do. Everyone goes to church. But only a small minority are living the [Christian] life seven days a week."

— *THE AUGUSTA CHRONICLE* (GEORGIA), MARCH 12, 1999

WON'T LIVING A GOOD LIFE SAVE OUR SOULS?

"A good life isn't going to save you. What will save you is the Cross."

— *ALBUQUERQUE JOURNAL* (NEW MEXICO), MAY 11, 1998

DOES EVERYONE NEED TO REPENT, EVEN GOOD PEOPLE?

"We're all sinners, and everyone who is in this place needs repentance and forgiveness, including me."

— SPEAKING AT THE FORTY-SIXTH ANNUAL NATIONAL PRAYER
BREAKFAST, *THE DALLAS MORNING NEWS*, FEBRUARY 6, 1998

SOMETIMES SIN HAPPENS GRADUALLY, LITTLE BY LITTLE, DOESN'T IT?

"You can take a frog and turn on hot water and he'll jump out. But put him in cold water and gradually turn the heat up and you can fry him. That's the way sin is. It comes on you so softly and so subtly you don't detect you're going down."

— *ST. PETERSBURG TIMES* (FLORIDA), OCTOBER 24, 1998

WHAT WAS YOUR REACTION WHEN THE KINSEY REPORT ON WOMEN WAS PUBLISHED IN 1953, FIVE YEARS AFTER THE ORIGINAL *SEXUAL BEHAVIOR IN THE HUMAN MALE*?

"It is impossible to estimate the damage this book will do to the already deteriorating morals of America."

— *THE GUARDIAN* (LONDON), OCTOBER 21, 1997

IS SEX AS WRONG A SIN AS SOME PEOPLE PREACH?

"As for sex, there's nothing wrong with it—as long as it takes place between a man and a woman who are married. It's the wrong use of sex that makes it a sin and makes it wrong."

— *THE DALLAS MORNING NEWS,* OCTOBER 18, 1997

ISN'T SEX GOD'S GIFT TO US?

"There's nothing wrong with sex. God gave us sex. None of us would be here tonight if it were not for sex. But there's a right way that God has outlined—within the bonds of matrimony."

— *FORT WORTH STAR-TELEGRAM* (TEXAS), OCTOBER 20, 2002

WHAT ARE YOUR VIEWS ON HOMOSEXUALITY? IS IT A SIN?

"The Bible says that homosexuality is wrong and it is a sin. Yet, God loves them and God accepts them."

— *ETHNIC NEWSWATCH,* SEPTEMBER 28, 1997

SOME PEOPLE SUGGEST THAT HOMOSEXUALITY IS ONE OF THE WORST SINS THAT PEOPLE CAN COMMIT. DO YOU AGREE?

"It is a sin. But there are other sins. Why do we jump on that sin as though it's the greatest sin?"

— *THE SAN FRANCISCO CHRONICLE,* SEPTEMBER 25, 1997

DO YOU LOVE HOMOSEXUALS DESPITE THEIR SIN?

"They have a lifestyle all their own; they have to make their own choice about it. It's not my lifestyle and it's certainly not the lifestyle of the Bible, but I love them and I'm very tolerant toward them."

— *ARKANSAS DEMOCRAT-GAZETTE* (LITTLE ROCK), SEPTEMBER 16, 1989

WHERE INSIDE OF US DOES EVIL RESIDE?

"The Bible says our hearts are a treasury of evil. . . . Evil thoughts come from the heart. You might commit adultery with your body, but it starts in the heart and in the mind. Our hearts are diseased by disease that the Bible calls sin. You see, the heart is also the seat of life. The Bible says your heart will live forever. Think of it: Your body is going to die and go to the grave, but your heart—your soul, your spirit—will live forever. A thousand years from tonight it will still be alive."

— *THE POST-STANDARD* (SYRACUSE, NY), APRIL 27, 1989

HOW DO YOU VIEW SEX FOR YOURSELF?

"When I was in high school and the early years of college, I was tempted so much so that I did not think I could hold on. But I turned it over to the Lord. And I never touched a woman in the wrong way . . . And the first time I ever had sex was the first night of my marriage. . . . And I can tell you one thing; it was worth it."

— *SAN JOSE MERCURY NEWS* (CALIFORNIA), SEPTEMBER 28, 1997

CAN YOU EVER GET SO FAR INTO SIN THAT GOD WILL FORGET YOU?

"I don't care how deep in sin you've gone. God loves you in everlasting love."

— *STAR TRIBUNE* (MINNEAPOLIS, MN), JUNE 18, 1996

WHAT WOULD YOU CONSIDER TO BE THE GREATEST MORAL IMPEDIMENT TO US REACHING GOD?

"Well, it's a three-letter word called sin, S-I-N. And that's the greatest impediment we have in the whole world today. And that's what is back of the wars, and that's what's back of broken homes, and that's what's back of all sorts of things."

—CNN's *LARRY KING LIVE*, DECEMBER 19, 1994

WHY IS BEING BORN AGAIN NECESSARY FOR A CHANGED LIFE?
"You can take a pig and clean him up and put him in your living room
. . . but open the door, and where does he go? Back to the mud hole,
because he feels more at home there. . . . Unless Christ changes one's
life, a person will sin and disobey God again."

— DURING A CRUSADE IN CLEVELAND, *PLAIN DEALER*
(CLEVELAND, OHIO), JUNE 10, 1994

ARE THOSE RESPONSIBLE FOR TV AND MOVIES PRODUCED IN
HOLLYWOOD WORSE SINNERS THAN THE REST OF US?
"We're all sinners. Everybody you meet all over the world is a sinner.
The word sin means you've broken with the laws of God. We've all
done that. So I couldn't condemn Hollywood Boulevard any more
than any other place . . . but I would call upon the industry today to
put more emphasis on moral and spiritual values."

— *LOS ANGELES TIMES*, OCTOBER 16, 1989

IS SOMETHING FUNDAMENTALLY WRONG WITH HUMAN
NATURE?
"What is the major cause of war, crime, divorce? All of these things
indicate that something is basically wrong with human nature. We're
all infected with this disease called sin."

— *THE TORONTO STAR*, OCTOBER 27, 1988

DOES GOD LOOK UPON US AS GROUPS OF SINNERS OR
INDIVIDUAL SINNERS?
"Man is a sinner. He needs a savior, he needs reconciling to God, and
God loves him. God looks upon you as an individual, not just as a
group of people. You are an individual who must stand before God
and give an account of your life."

— PR NEWSWIRE, SEPTEMBER 8, 1988

WILL WE ALL EVENTUALLY HAVE TO PAY FOR OUR SINS?

"There are people today who literally live for pleasure. Many people live their lives like that. They can hardly wait for the weekend to go out drinking and partying. But know this, pay day is coming."

— THE ASSOCIATED PRESS STATE & LOCAL WIRE, JUNE 23, 2001

CAN JESUS REALLY HELP OUR SEX LIVES?

"Accepting Christ may not change your circumstances, but he can change you from the inside. You'll have new perspective on life, a new inner strength. He can help you in your sex life. There's nothing wrong with sex. God gave it to us, within the bonds of matrimony. But if you have committed that sin, bring it to Christ. He can give you new life."

— *ASHEVILLE CITIZEN-TIMES* (NORTH CAROLINA), JUNE 30, 2002

YOU OFTEN TELL YOUNGER PEOPLE THAT REPENTING FOR YOUR SINS IS LIKE RESTARTING A COMPUTER. HOW SO?

"When a computer is locked up, you can push control, alt, delete and start all over again. . . . You can do that tonight. You can push the control button. It's the opening of a new document."

— *DAILY OKLAHOMAN* (OKLAHOMA CITY), JUNE 15, 2003

YOU'VE LIKENED "UNSEEN SIN" TO A DIAMOND. WHAT DID YOU MEAN BY THAT?

"A diamond may be perfect to a natural eye, but you take it to a specialist and he looks at it through a glass and sees a defect in it. And God looks at us that way."

— *LOS ANGELES TIMES*, NOVEMBER 19, 2004

IS BIGOTRY A SIN?

"We need to do everything we can to be friends and neighbors to those chosen by God to be his people. . . . Bigotry of any kind is a sin in God's eyes."

— *THE AUGUSTA CHRONICLE* (GEORGIA). JUNE 30, 2002;

ASHEVILLE CITIZEN-TIMES, JUNE 29, 2002

What Billy Graham and the Billy Graham Evangelistic Association Believe

The Bible to be the infallible Word of God, that it is His holy and inspired Word, and that it is of supreme and final authority.

In one God, eternally existing in three persons—Father, Son, and Holy Spirit.

Jesus Christ was conceived by the Holy Spirit, born of the Virgin Mary. He led a sinless life, took on Himself all our sins, died and rose again, and is seated at the right hand of the Father as our mediator and advocate.

That all men everywhere are lost and face the judgment of God, and need to come to a saving knowledge of Jesus Christ through His shed blood on the cross.

That Christ rose from the dead and is coming soon.

In holy Christian living, and that we must have concern for the hurts and social needs of our fellowmen.

We must dedicate ourselves anew to the service of our Lord and to His authority over our lives.

In using every modern means of communication available to us to spread the Gospel of Jesus Christ throughout the world.

On Technology
and Religion

Is technology the answer to all our problems, as
many people think?
"Technology doesn't solve all problems. . . . Death is still inevitable,
though technology projects the myth of control over our own mortality."

— Speaking at Harvard University, University Wire, September 28, 1999

Will technology change society as many people
suggest?
"Some of the things I've heard are going to happen technologically
are way beyond anything I can think about. I don't think that's going
to change society. Society is made up of people, and people are the
same the world over."

— Lansing State Journal, December 26, 1999

Is technology a panacea for the world's ills?
"The technology that was supposed to save us is now ready to destroy
us. Germ and chemical warfare threaten the fragile balance of peace
in the world. In face of these terrors, we have a hope. Jesus is already
getting ready to go back to the Father."

— The Ottawa Sun, June 29, 1998

IS TECHNOLOGY PUSHING OUT RELIGION FOR PEOPLE'S
ATTENTION?

"The information age may go down in history as the period when our
culture forgot the most important thing: That our souls need to
breathe and grow. We're separated from God. We're dead people
walking."

—THE CANADIAN PRESS, JUNE 25, 1998

TECHNOLOGY IS A TWO-EDGED SWORD, ISN'T IT?

"It is amazing how technology is being used to hurt the world. But it
is also being used to spread the Gospel on a scale that has never happened in the history of the Christian church."

—PR NEWSWIRE, OCTOBER 14, 1998

HOW CAN TECHNOLOGY HELP PEOPLE WITH PREACHING?

"At my age, I would like to just sit in a study somewhere and preach
through this new electronic equipment they have now—the Internet.
You can touch the world from just one place."

—*THE TIMES UNION* (ALBANY, NY), JUNE 8, 1997

WHY DID YOU BUILD A WEB SITE FOR THE BILLY GRAHAM
EVANGELISTIC ASSOCIATION?

"The technology revolution has shrunk the world to a global village,
with instant access to world news networks in even the most remote
areas. It is time for the church to utilize this technology to make a
worldwide statement that in the midst of chaos, emptiness and
despair, there is hope in the person of Jesus Christ."

—COX NEWS SERVICE, SEPTEMBER 24, 1997

WHAT PIECE OF TECHNOLOGY HAS ALLOWED YOUR MINISTRY
TO MAKE THE GREATEST IMPACT?

"Through this World Television Series, we anticipate reaching 2.5 billion people, most of whom we could never reach in our usual crusade ministry. I believe this will have a far greater impact than anything we have ever done before."

—ON THE TV SHOW THAT WAS AIRED AT PRIME TIME DURING APRIL IN
MORE THAN TWO HUNDRED COUNTRIES AND DESIGNED TO APPEAL TO A YOUNGER,
MEDIA-SAVVY, INTERNATIONAL AUDIENCE. PR NEWSWIRE, APRIL 9, 1996

HOW CAN YOU USE TELEVISION TO BALANCE OUT THE
NEGATIVE MESSAGES THIS MEDIA OFTEN BROADCASTS?

"Television brings stories of pain and suffering, violence and crime into our homes every day. There's not a better time than now to use the same technology to bring a message of hope."

—SPEAKING ABOUT THE GLOBAL MISSION, BROADCAST WORLDWIDE FROM THE
GREATER PUERTO RICO BILLY GRAHAM CRUSADE IN SAN JUAN. SATELLITE UPLINKS
TRANSMITTED TO LOCAL SITES IN 175 COUNTRIES, REACHING UP TO EIGHT MILLION
PEOPLE NIGHTLY IN WHAT GRAHAM ESTIMATED WOULD BE THE GREATEST GOSPEL
OUTREACH IN HISTORY. *THE EVENING POST* (WELLINGTON), MARCH 15, 1995

HOW DOES REACHING OUT TO MILLIONS OF PEOPLE
WORLDWIDE THROUGH TELEVISION MAKE YOU FEEL?

"In some ways, I feel like the old-fashioned circuit riders, such as John Wesley in England and his counterparts in early America, who rode on horseback from town to town to preach the Gospel. Now through state-of-the-art technology via satellite, we can become 'electronic circuit riders' and reach thousands of venues at the same time."

—PR NEWSWIRE, MARCH 10, 1995

IS TELEVISION PREACHING LESS PERSONAL THAN YOU'D LIKE?
"It's not television. It's as though I am coming to a place personally."

— *THE RECORD* (KITCHENER-WATERLOO, ONTARIO), MARCH 4, 1995

WHY WAS THE TIME RIPE FOR GLOBAL MISSION IN 1995?
"Our homes are confused, mixed up and broken. There are wars going on—or seemingly about to break out—all over the world. This is a very strategic moment to get before people and tell them that God loves them, that God has a plan and that God is interested in them. That is what we're planning to do through Global Mission."

— PR NEWSWIRE, FEBRUARY 21, 1995

HOW CAN TECHNOLOGY HELP SPREAD THE WORD OF JESUS CHRIST TO REMOTE AREAS OF THE WORLD?
"The technology revolution has shrunk the world to a global village, with instant access to world news networks in even the most remote areas. It is time for the church to use this technology to make a worldwide statement that in the midst of chaos, emptiness and despair, there is hope in the person of Jesus Christ."

— PR NEWSWIRE, JANUARY 5, 1995

HOW DOES TECHNOLOGY HELP YOU SPREAD THE GOSPEL?
"By using new technologies, I feel we can reach more people in the future than we have been able to reach in the past. We are grateful for opportunities to present the Prince of Peace and His power to transform lives and society."

— PR NEWSWIRE, DECEMBER 22, 1995

WHAT MESSAGE DO YOU HAVE FOR THOSE IN THE MEDIA
ABOUT THEIR RESPONSIBILITY FOR PRODUCING MORAL
ENTERTAINMENT?

"Technology has given us the tools to touch the world for good or
evil. Unfortunately, a great deal of our entertainment is filled with
violence, sex and drugs. I would call on the industry today to put far
more emphasis on moral and spiritual values and bring our programs
more into conformity with the Ten Commandments. In light of
recent headlines, I would say we of the Church need to join the
entertainment industry in changing."

—PR NEWSWIRE, OCTOBER 16, 1989

FROM WHERE CAN WE GET THE STRENGTH TO CONTROL
TECHNOLOGY, SUCH AS NUCLEAR BOMBS, THAT CAN GREATLY
HARM US?

"We need the moral ability to control technology and I am of the
opinion that Christ can give it."

—UNITED PRESS INTERNATIONAL, SEPTEMBER 19, 1984

IS IT A MYTH TO THINK THAT TECHNOLOGY CAN GIVE US
MORE TIME?

"The word 'perplexed' means no way out. The word 'distress' means
to be pressed from all sides. And that's the way we are today. We're
pressed from all sides. People are having nervous breakdowns and
don't know why. . . . We live in a pressure-cooked society. We've
invented all these things to save our time, and we don't have any time."

—*THE DALLAS MORNING NEWS,* JUNE 22, 2001

On THE UNITED STATES AND THE AMERICAN PEOPLE

EVERY SO OFTEN THE UNITED STATES GETS OFF TRACK. WHAT DID YOU SAY DURING ONE OF THESE PERIODS?

"Our world is growing more dangerous and chaotic every day. If ever there was a time for the American people to repent of sin and trust in God, it is now."

— ASSOCIATED PRESS, APRIL 25, 1980

WHAT DOES A MULTICULTURAL SOCIETY LIKE THE UNITED STATES NEED TO SURVIVE AND PROSPER?

"This country is no longer a country of one faith. We all need a certain amount of tolerance if we're going to get along with each other. We're to love one another."

— *THE COMMERCIAL APPEAL* (MEMPHIS, TN), JUNE 2, 2000

HAVE YOU SEEN A CHANGE IN PEOPLE'S ATTITUDES TOWARD CONSUMERISM?

"A revolt is rising against materialism. The whole world is asking questions about the West's lifestyle of affluence. It doesn't satisfy spiritually. Materialism is not the answer to man's greatest need. Only God is."

— ASSOCIATED PRESS, JANUARY 25, 1980

DO YOU SEE MORE AMERICANS MOVING TOWARD CHRIST?
"I see people believing more and more and more in Christ. Maybe not to surrender their lives to him, but they believe he is the only answer to life's problems."

— ASSOCIATED PRESS, DECEMBER 15, 1999

WHAT IS THE GREATEST SPIRITUAL THREAT FACING THE UNITED STATES?
"As a nation we are in danger of leaving God out of our lives. We need a spiritual awakening."

— DURING A CRUSADE IN TAMPA, *ST. PETERSBURG TIMES* (FLORIDA), OCTOBER 26, 1998

YOU'VE SAID THAT AMERICANS HAVE CONFUSED LICENSE WITH LIBERTY. WHAT DID YOU MEAN BY THAT?
"There is much about America that is no longer good. . . . Racial and ethnic tensions that threaten to rip apart our neighborhoods. Crime and violence of epidemic proportions. Children bringing weapons to school. Broken families. Poverty. The whole list is known to us. . . . We've confused liberty with license and we're paying the awful price. We're a society poised on the brink of self-destruction unless God intervenes and helps us."

— SPEAKING BEFORE A JOINT SESSION OF THE NORTH CAROLINA LEGISLATURE, *THE CHARLOTTE OBSERVER* (NORTH CAROLINA), MAY 6, 1997

HOW IMPORTANT ARE RACE RELATIONS TO AMERICA'S SURVIVAL?
"The sharp racial division over the O.J. Simpson trials demonstrates
the deep need for racial reconciliation in America. Racial reconciliation is one of our greatest problems as a nation."

—*SAN ANTONIO EXPRESS-NEWS* (TEXAS). MARCH 2. 1997

WHAT HAS HAPPENED IN THE UNITED STATES IN PARTICULAR
SINCE WORLD WAR II THAT TROUBLES YOU?
"The real problem is within ourselves. After World War II, America
had the opportunity to rule the world. Instead, we turned away from
that and helped rebuild the countries of our enemies. Nevertheless,
something has happened since those days and there is much about
America which is no longer good. . . . We must turn around and
change roads. If ever we needed God's hope, it's now. If ever we
needed spiritual renewal, it's now."

—UPON RECEIVING THE CONGRESSIONAL GOLD MEDAL.

STATES NEWS SERVICE. MAY 2. 1996

HOW DID YOU DESCRIBE THE "DISCONNECT" BETWEEN
BELIEVING GOD AND OBEYING HIS COMMANDMENTS?
"While many Americans believe there is a God, most have not
accepted true Christianity or Judaism or Islam. They believe the Bible,
but they don't read it or obey it."

—*ROCKY MOUNTAIN NEWS* (DENVER. CO). APRIL 3. 1994

WHAT'S MISSING FROM AMERICAN LIFE COMPARED TO THE
WAY IT WAS WHEN YOU WERE YOUNG?
"I think people are distracted today by all the sports and all the entertainment that saturates the atmosphere and people don't have time anymore. We don't have time anymore to sit down and quietly spend time
with our families like we used to. I remember in our neighborhood were

families that never went out in the evenings, and they would sit and read and talk about some novel. And the Bible was always a part of it."

— *THE TIMES UNION* (ALBANY, NY), AUGUST 27, 1994

YOU'VE ADVOCATED CORPORAL PUNISHMENT FOR SOME
CRIMES. WHY?

"Our judicial system is going to have to be revised and changed, and we're going to have to have some corporal punishment that even our young people will understand. . . . There is a difference between punishment and torture. . . . Crime has become our No. 1 problem. I have talked to all kinds of people and they agree something has to be done."

— DURING AN INTERVIEW AT THE DEDICATION OF THE BILLY GRAHAM

CENTER MUSEUM AT WHEATON COLLEGE, *CHICAGO SUN-TIMES,* MAY 12, 1994

HAVE AMERICAN VALUES BEEN TURNED UPSIDE DOWN?

"America has undergone an inversion of values in the 20th century. That which was once considered bad is now accepted and even celebrated. Young people today are especially affected by the deterioration of the moral and spiritual foundation of our society. So many children grow up without the moral authority of parents, and every day we read of lives marred by abuse, drugs, alcohol and sexually transmitted diseases."

— *CALL AND POST* (COLUMBUS, OH), OCTOBER 7, 1993

WHAT CAN WE DO TO CHANGE TELEVISION PROGRAMMING
THAT WE DON'T LIKE?

"The lack of primetime piety is evidence of a cultural breakdown, and a loss of moral values and ideals that enable a democracy to function. As viewers, we need to let the [television] industry know how much it means to us when programs depict our Judeo-Christian values."

— ON THERE NOT BEING ENOUGH MORAL ROLE MODELS

IN PRIME-TIME TELEVISION SHOWS, *USA TODAY,* JULY 12, 1993

CAN PEOPLE BE LONELY EVEN IN LARGE METROPOLITAN
AREAS LIKE NEW YORK CITY?
"Everybody I talk to, it seems, agrees that New York is the loneliest
place in the world. People get increasingly irritable and pushy in their
effort to guard their own turf. There's little space for others, let alone
God. To be without God in New York is to be terribly lonely."

—IN A SERMON TO PEOPLE GATHERED IN CENTRAL PARK, QUOTED IN

THE ATLANTA JOURNAL AND CONSTITUTION, SEPTEMBER 23, 1991

YOU SPOKE IN NEW YORK CITY DURING A TOUGH TIME FOR
THE CITY AS FAR AS CRIME, RACIAL TENSIONS, AND FINANCIAL
CHALLENGES WERE CONCERNED. WHAT WAS YOUR MESSAGE TO
THE 250,000 PEOPLE WHO HEARD YOU SPEAK?
"I think that if the people will do what they did 150 years ago—turn
back to God and have a great spiritual awakening—it would certainly help solve the problems that they are facing. I talked to the
mayor about it a couple of times and several of the leaders of this city
and the Jewish rabbis. I've been here nearly a month going around
to different events and receptions and to parties, even, and met a lot
of people, and we have talked about that. What could happen—and
here in 1857, they started a prayer meeting on Fulton Street and
Wall Street. And out of that little prayer meeting of six, it grew and
grew and grew until it spread all over the country, and it changed
New York."

—*CBS THIS MORNING,* SEPTEMBER 23, 1991

ON WHAT DOES THE FUTURE OF AMERICA HINGE?

"Unless moral and spiritual values are strengthened in government, education, management, labor, the mass media, the family, and the church, the free way of life we have known in the modern world, the Western World, may be in danger. Whether or not we turn out to be great as a nation, depends on how we treat the laws of God."

—PR NEWSWIRE, APRIL 8, 1991

ARE YOU SAYING THAT AMERICA IS DOOMED?

"I'm convinced that unless our moral and spiritual values are strengthened in government, education, management, labor, the mass media, sports and in every area of society, then the free way we have known in this country may be doomed."

—PR NEWSWIRE, APRIL 25, 1989

DO YOU THINK THAT WASHINGTON, DC IS A BELLWETHER FOR THE REST OF THE UNITED STATES?

"Washington, with its sins, its drunkenness, its crime, will prove the test of what is going to happen to America. Despite the tremendous unique influences and contributions of Washington, in many ways it mirrors—sometimes in stark detail—many of the problems of our entire nation, such as poverty and the homeless, widespread drug abuse, corruption, the breakup of families and loneliness."

—THREE DAYS BEFORE THE OPENING OF A CRUSADE IN WASHINGTON, DC. *LOS ANGELES TIMES*, APRIL 26, 1986

WASHINGTON, DC IS THE CAPITAL OF THE MOST POWERFUL
AND WEALTHIEST NATION THE WORLD HAS EVER SEEN;
SHOULDN'T IT BE A MODEL FOR THE REST OF THE WORLD?
"Surely it is hollow to talk about great ideals such as justice and mercy
and equal opportunity in our world when within a mile of the United
States Capitol building those are often not practiced."

—UNITED PRESS INTERNATIONAL, MAY 1, 1985

HOW HAVE YOUR VIEWS CHANGED ON BELIEVING THAT THE
AMERICAN WAY OF LIFE SHOULD BE EMULATED AROUND THE
WORLD?
"In the '50s I used to make the mistake of almost identifying the
Kingdom of God with the American Way of Life. . . . I felt that the
American way of life of course was the best life in the whole world,
and the whole world ought to adopt our way of life. I've come to see
that other cultures have their own way of life that may be of just as
great a value to them as our way of life to us."

—ASSOCIATED PRESS, FEBRUARY 1, 1980

HAVE WE AS A NATION GONE TOO FAR IN TAKING GOD OUT
OF OUR PUBLIC INSTITUTIONS?
"There is a great move going on in this country to take prayer out of
the schools, take God out of the pledge of allegiance, and take down
the Ten Commandments. As a nation it seems we are turning away
from God."

—PR NEWSWIRE, OCTOBER 11, 2004

On THE LIFE OF
JESUS CHRIST

IN YOUR OPINION, WHAT WAS JESUS CHRIST'S ULTIMATE
PURPOSE IN LIFE?
"He fed the poor. He healed the sick, raised the dead, but that was
not his purpose. His purpose was to go to the cross."

—St. Louis Post-Dispatch (Missouri), October 18, 1999

SOME PEOPLE DIVIDE JESUS' LIFE INTO SEPARATE TIME
PERIODS. DO YOU THINK THAT IS VALID?
"There are three things that I think you can't separate in the life of
Jesus Christ. One is the cradle—his birth—and the next thing is the
cross where he died for our sins, and the third is the resurrection."

—CNN's Larry King Live, December 25, 1998

WHAT ARE THE TWO ROADS OF LIFE THAT JESUS TAUGHT US?
"Jesus taught that there are two roads of life. Many of you are in the
ruts of life and you just keep on going and you don't change. But
there's a highway that God has built for us. He offers us an opportunity to get out of those ruts and to get on a magnificent freeway, a
diamond lane that will take you to heaven. Death is not our final des-

tination, only the doorway to it. Only those prepared to die are really prepared to live."

—PR NEWSWIRE, OCTOBER 17, 1997

WHAT HAS JESUS TOLD US ABOUT THE END OF TIME?
"The Bible is very clear that someday history as we know it will come to an end, and Christ will come again to establish his Kingdom of justice and righteousness. But Christ also warned us against speculating about the exact time this will happen. Our responsibility is to be ready for that day—for someday he will come."

—*COLUMBUS DISPATCH* (OHIO), MARCH 16, 1995

WHAT'S THE IMPORTANCE OF ACCEPTING THE MIRACLES THAT JESUS PERFORMED?
"We have to go back to the basics. Jesus performed miracles to prove his divinity, and so I accept them, and I accept them by faith. I can't prove everything scientifically. But when I do accept the Scriptures by faith, it has an impact in my own personal life, and I can apply the principles Jesus taught to every life. So to me the miracles of Christ are essential. They are not only essential to salvation, but to one's Christian living."

—*OTTAWA CITIZEN*, DECEMBER 23, 1995

WHAT TEXT HAVE YOU DESCRIBED AS A "MINIATURE GOSPEL"?
"For God so loved the world that he gave his only begotten Son, that whosoever believeth in him should not perish, but have everlasting life. . . . The text is only 25 words, but it is like a miniature Gospel."

—READING FROM JOHN 3:16, OPENING A FIVE-DAY CRUSADE IN PITTSBURGH'S THREE RIVERS STADIUM. *PLAIN DEALER* (CLEVELAND, OHIO), JUNE 3, 1993

IS JESUS STILL LIVING?

"Jesus Christ is not dead on the cross. He is a living Christ. He can come to your person. He can come to your family. He can come to your great country."

—DURING A TRIP TO THE SOVIET UNION.
UNITED PRESS INTERNATIONAL. MAY 19, 1985

WHY DID GOD SEND HIS SON TO US?

"God had a son, and he sent him to rescue us, to save us. I remember one time, I was walking with one of my sons. We stepped on an anthill and some of the ants were dying and some were wounded. . . . And I said, 'Wouldn't it be wonderful if we could go down there and help those ants and tell them that we didn't mean to do that.' And my son said: 'Dad, we can't. We're too big. They're too little.' And I said, 'That's exactly what God was. God became man.'"

—*THE DALLAS MORNING NEWS*. OCTOBER 18, 2002

HOW DID YOU FEEL AFTER YOU SAW MEL GIBSON'S CONTROVERSIAL FILM *THE PASSION OF THE CHRIST*?

"I was moved to tears. I have often wondered what it must have been like to be a bystander during those last hours before Jesus' death. After watching the film, I feel as if I have actually been there. . . . No one who views this film's compelling imagery will ever be the same again. . . . It was faithful to the Bible's teaching. I doubt if there has been a more graphic and moving presentation of Jesus' death and resurrection, which Christians believe are the most important events in human history. . . . The film is faithful to the Bible's teaching that we are all responsible for Jesus' death because we have all sinned. It is our sins that caused his death, not any particular group."

—*THE JEWISH WEEK*. DECEMBER 5, 2003

ALTHOUGH JESUS WAS ONLY ON THE EARTH FOR A SHORT
TIME, HOW WOULD YOU DESCRIBE HIS NOTORIETY?

"Jesus is the best known person that ever lived. He did more in the
thirty-three years that he lived than all the rest of the leaders in history put together. He stood up in front of all the people who stood
mocking him, murdering him, and he said, 'I forgive them.' He said
that to the whole world. He said, 'I love you.'"

— *THE FLORIDA TIMES-UNION* (JACKSONVILLE), JUNE 24, 2005

Billy Graham's
Official Position
on Politics
from the Billy Graham
Evangelistic Association

It is true that many, many years ago Mr. Graham registered as a Democrat. However, throughout the years he has voted for the candidate he believes will do the best job. In other words, he has not voted a straight party ticket. Mr. Graham takes his responsibility to vote for the leaders of our country with the same prayerful seriousness that he takes other significant decisions.

Mr. Graham has always maintained an optimistic attitude toward people. He seeks the good and emphasizes what is positive, even if he does not agree with them on many points, including moral or political issues. Mr. Graham's comments sometimes are not presented in the complete context in which they were made; while at other times, he himself would perhaps wish he might have phrased things a bit differently. However, he does not presently and never has condoned or defended immoral conduct.

Mr. Graham's lifelong calling has been to proclaim the gospel of our Lord and Savior Jesus Christ throughout the world. As you are aware, he has been faithful to this mission. He has not compromised his message.

On WAR AND PEACE

WHAT ARE YOUR THOUGHTS ON THE USE OF NUCLEAR WEAPONS?
"I am not a pacifist and I don't believe in unilateral disarmament, but I do believe in the destruction of nuclear weapons. As long as any of these weapons exist there is a danger to the world."

— *THE WASHINGTON POST*, DECEMBER 14, 1981

WHAT WOULD BE THE OUTCOME OF A NUCLEAR WAR?
"The only monument after a nuclear war will not be a few acres of well-tended ground but an entire planet, charred and lifeless because we did not have the vision and moral courage to destroy all weapons of mass destruction."

— UNITED PRESS INTERNATIONAL, NOVEMBER 4, 1982

CAN WE LEARN ABOUT THE HORROR OF WAR FROM CITIES LIKE LIDICE?
"Lidice should stand as a sober warning of what might happen to our world if we do not find a way to reduce the terrible threat of weapons of mass destruction. . . . I pray that our world will never become another Lidice."

— UPON LAYING A WREATH AT THE MEMORIAL TO THE VICTIMS OF A
NAZI MASSACRE DURING WORLD WAR II IN LIDICE, CZECHOSLOVAKIA,
ABOUT TWELVE MILES FROM PRAGUE, ASSOCIATED PRESS, NOVEMBER 2, 1982

WHAT IS THE WORLD'S COMMON ENEMY?

"Our common enemy is the threat of impending nuclear destruction. Policies which constantly take nations to the brink of nuclear war must be rejected."

—BBC SUMMARY OF WORLD BROADCASTS, MAY 17, 1982

IS IT HUMANITY'S LOT TO ALWAYS ENDURE WAR?

"I think there is going to be, according to prophecies of the Bible, wars and rumors of wars until the end of time. And I don't think there is anything that can change that, except the human heart, because I think the change has to come from within us. And, it is not the guns, it is not the atomic bombs, that do the harm. It is the people that build them and it is people that pull the triggers and push the buttons."

—CNN *LARRY KING LIVE*, DECEMBER 31, 1999

CAN WE EVER STOP WAR THROUGH PRAYER?

"Fifteen nations now have the atomic bomb. It could fall into the hands of a terrorist group. . . . And the only way that we can stop war is through prayer."

—ASSOCIATED PRESS, FEBRUARY 13, 1987

WHAT'S THE TRUE COST TO THE WORLD OF EXORBITANT MILITARY SPENDING?

"How can we be indifferent to the millions and millions who live on the brink of starvation each year, while the nations of the world spend $550 billion each year on weapons?"

—FACTS ON FILE *WORLD NEWS DIGEST*, FEBRUARY 13, 1981

HOW CAN WE ACHIEVE WORLD PEACE?

"Humans need to be changed before we can really see peace. Wars are started in the human heart."

—UNITED PRESS INTERNATIONAL, OCTOBER 25, 1982

IS WAR UNAVOIDABLE?

"The whole world wants peace, yet somehow or other in almost every generation we stumble into war. . . . It all comes back to man. It's in our hearts—our hearts must be changed."

—UNITED PRESS INTERNATIONAL, OCTOBER 21, 1982

WHAT IS YOUR HOPE FOR MIDDLE EAST PEACE INITIATIVES?

"Mothers, fathers and grandparents have lost family members and are hurting. Many biblical events took place in the part of the world where the present disputes are occurring. As Christians, we should be praying for peace and reconciliation. Centuries ago, the Apostle Paul called for reconciliation between Jews and Gentiles. I am praying for, and supporting the efforts among leaders of both sides being undertaken in Egypt."

—*ASHEVILLE CITIZEN-TIMES*, OCTOBER 20, 2000

YOU SAY THAT SATAN AND HIS DEMONS DON'T GET ENOUGH ATTENTION FOR SOME OF THE WORLD'S HORRIFIC WARS LIKE THE GENOCIDE IN KOSOVO. HOW DO WE FIGHT THE DEVIL?

"We are in a spiritual warfare and we can't fight the devil with carnal weapons. We can't take rifles and shoot him. We have to fight him on a spiritual level, and that means more prayer and more study of the Word of God and more faithfulness in our fellowship with each other in the church."

—PR NEWSWIRE, JUNE 7, 1999

WHAT HAS SADDENED YOU ABOUT THE TWENTIETH CENTURY?

"As we march into the new century, there's great uncertainty and fear. . . . This was supposed to be the Christian century, but we had two world wars in which more people were killed than there had been in several centuries combined."

—*SAN ANTONIO EXPRESS-NEWS* (TEXAS), APRIL 7, 1997

WHAT IS THE RELIGIOUS LEGACY OF THOSE WHO FOUGHT IN
WORLD WAR II?

"I can't help but think how many of those men risked their lives and
gave their lives in order that we might have meetings like this. . . .
Those who stormed the beaches were under orders from their
Commander-in-Chief. . . . The Lord, my commander in chief, has
commanded me to preach the Gospel around the world."

—PR NEWSWIRE, JUNE 7, 1994

DO ORDINARY PEOPLE HAVE ANY INFLUENCE ON WORLD PEACE?

"I am convinced that ordinary people can have an influence on world
peace. The greatest contribution we can possibly make is that we ourselves have peace. Most of us have little wars going on inside, or in
our families, or our communities or our schools. That's what the
Gospel is all about—to reconcile us to God. To have peace within
ourselves is a tremendous thing in the world in which we live, and it
has a great impact on people around us."

—PR NEWSWIRE, NOVEMBER 1, 1993

WHY IS THERE SO MUCH VIOLENCE IN THE WORLD?

"People often ask me why there is so much violence in the world.
Although South Africa has been in the headlines, you are by no
means alone in facing violence. At this moment, literally dozens of
countries are wracked by warfare and conflict. In my own country we
have had over 25,000 murders since the beginning of the year—a terrible toll. As hard as it may be for us to admit it to ourselves, injus-
tice, prejudice, violence and hatred all come ultimately from within
us—from our hearts and our minds. But, it doesn't have to be that
way, and the reason is because God loves us and He wants to change
our hearts. The Bible says there can be peace."

—IN A MESSAGE BROADCAST BY THE SOUTH AFRICAN BROADCASTING
COMPANY TO PEOPLE IN SOUTH AFRICA, PR NEWSWIRE, SEPTEMBER 19, 1991

WAS THE FIRST GULF WAR JUSTIFIED?
"I'm against all war and believe in peace. But, there comes a time—
as St. Augustine long ago said—when there is a just war; where you
have to choose between two evils. I think this was a just war."

—PR NEWSWIRE, APRIL 2, 1991

DO YOU BELIEVE IN THE NEW WORLD ORDER?
"There come times when we have to fight for peace. . . . Out of the
war may come a new peace and, as suggested by the President, a new
world order."

—*LOS ANGELES TIMES*, FEBRUARY 2, 1991

ARE YOU SOMETIMES FRUSTRATED AT THE HUMAN RACE FOR
THE VIOLENCE THAT PEOPLE COMMIT?
"This was to have been the Christian century. But it has been any-
thing but the Christian century. What's wrong with the human race?
Why can we never settle our problems peacefully?"

—DURING A NON-DENOMINATIONAL CHURCH SERVICE ARRANGED
BY GRAHAM AT THE CHAPEL IN FORT MYER, VIRGINIA,
OUTSIDE OF WASHINGTON, DC, SHORTLY AFTER THE START OF THE
GULF WAR. *ST. PETERSBURG TIMES* (FLORIDA), JANUARY 18, 1991

IS WAR SOMETIMES NECESSARY TO PROTECT THOSE WHO ARE
WEAK OR OPPRESSED?
"No sane person wants war. At the same time, it has been well said
that there is an ethical responsibility that goes with power, and sometimes it becomes necessary to fight the strong in order to protect
the weak."

—REFERRING TO THE FIRST GULF WAR, ASSOCIATED PRESS, JANUARY 10, 1991

YOU'VE EXPRESSED CONCERN THAT THE "FINAL WAR" COULD
COME IN THE MIDDLE EAST BASED ON BIBLICAL PROPHECIES.
WHAT ARE YOUR THOUGHTS ABOUT THAT?
"There are spiritual forces at work there. I can't answer what they are,
but they are at work and it is not going to be a usual type of situation. It's going to be something we have not seen in our century
before. . . . History has gone full circle, and we are coming back to
these [Bible] lands. This is not another Korea, it is not another
Vietnam—it is something far more sinister and far more difficult."

—PREACHING TO A CROWD AT A FIVE-DAY CRUSADE THAT SET ATTENDANCE
RECORDS AT NASSAU COLISEUM IN LONG ISLAND, NEW YORK, *U.S. NEWS & WORLD
REPORT*, NOVEMBER 19, 1990; UNITED PRESS INTERNATIONAL NOVEMBER 9, 1990

CAN WE BE AT PEACE WITH EACH OTHER IF WE'RE NOT AT
PEACE WITH GOD?
"There is a difference between 'peace' and 'the lessening of hostili-
ties.' Men and nations are not at peace with each other, because they
are not at peace with God. Man cannot deliver peace on earth, only
God can."

—PR NEWSWIRE, DECEMBER 20, 1988

WILL GOD HELP US PREVENT ARMAGEDDON?
"I do not believe that peace is going to come through our own efforts.
I think God is going to intervene. And as we stand on the brink of
Armageddon, God will intervene. The Prince of Peace is going to
come back and we are going to have peace on earth when Christ
reigns. Until then, we have every responsibility to work for peace, to
pray for peace."

—*THE TORONTO STAR*, FEBRUARY 15, 1986

WHAT'S THE EMOTIONAL AND PSYCHOLOGICAL EFFECT ON
YOUNG PEOPLE OF LIVING UNDER A CLOUD OF POSSIBLE
NUCLEAR WAR?

"Each day the crisis multiplies. Each day the solution grows more difficult. Each day we grow nearer the hour of maximum danger, as weapons spread and hostile forces grow stronger. Think of the psychological impact that is on the emerging generation—a nuclear cloud hanging over their head. And they're not sure if they'll be able to live normal lives."

—AT A PRAYER BREAKFAST AT THE NATIONAL GOVERNORS' ASSOCIATION
CONFERENCE IN BOISE, IDAHO, UNITED PRESS INTERNATIONAL, AUGUST 5, 1985

DURING THE COLD WAR, WERE YOU MORE CONCERNED ABOUT
THE SUPERPOWERS OR SMALLER COUNTRIES STARTING A
NUCLEAR WAR?

"I am not so much worried about the Soviet Union and the United States. I am worried about smaller nations that could get a bomb and start a chain reaction."

—UNITED PRESS INTERNATIONAL, SEPTEMBER 11, 1984

IS IT GOD'S WILL IF WE HAVE A NUCLEAR WAR?

"I know that man himself is responsible for his actions. We have become giants technologically but morally and spiritually we are pygmies. If the nuclear button is pressed, it will be a human being who presses it. The ultimate problem is within man's hearts."

—UNITED PRESS INTERNATIONAL, SEPTEMBER 11, 1984

IF WE WERE TO HAVE A NUCLEAR WAR, WOULD THE ENTIRE
WORLD BE DESTROYED ACCORDING TO SCRIPTURE?

"With the proliferation of nuclear weapons, the destruction of the world could come at any time. But the Bible teaches that we're not going to destroy ourselves as a human race. Maybe a fourth of the human race, or more . . . but God has plans for this world, to bring peace and justice and He is going to rule."

—UNITED PRESS INTERNATIONAL, NOVEMBER 7, 1983

WE ALL PRAY THAT NUCLEAR WAR NEVER HAPPENS, BUT HOW CAN WE PREPARE OURSELVES IF THE WORST SHOULD HAPPEN?
"Who knows when some wild Hitler will come and push the button that starts the chain reaction, so that you can't make your plans for the future? But there's one thing you can do. You can have the peace with God and the peace of God in your heart now, to meet whatever eventuality there is."

—DURING A SPEAKING TOUR OF NEW ENGLAND COLLEGES,

THE NEW YORK TIMES, APRIL 16, 1982

WHAT WAS YOUR STANCE ON THE VIETNAM WAR?
"I don't ever recall making a statement supporting the Vietnam War or being against it. I just didn't take a position. And I was kicked by both sides—hawks and doves."

—ASSOCIATED PRESS, AUGUST 7, 1979

WAS IT A MISTAKE TO DEVELOP THE ATOMIC BOMB?
"I'm in favor of disarmament and I'm in favor of trust. I'm in favor of having agreements not only to reduce, but to eliminate [nuclear weapons]. Why should any nation have atomic bombs? As I look back—and I'm sure many people will disagree with me on this—but as I look back, I think Mr. Truman made a mistake in dropping that first atomic bomb. I wish we'd never developed it."

—*THE WASHINGTON POST*, JUNE 29, 1979, CITING

AN APPEARANCE ON THE *CBS EVENING NEWS*

HAVE THE TERRORIST ATTACKS OF 9/11 HAD AN EFFECT ON
PEOPLE'S SPIRITUALITY?

"During the three months since the attacks on New York and
Washington, there has been an unprecedented search for purpose and
meaning in our troubled world. This is especially true in a large metropolitan community such as Dallas–Ft. Worth, which is a leading
area in our country today and will be on into the future." *(On
announcing an evangelistic mission in the Metroplex at Texas Stadium)*

—PR NEWSWIRE, DECEMBER 20, 2001

WHAT ADVICE DID YOU OFFER TO PEOPLE WHO WERE
WORRIED AFTER THE 9/11 TERRORIST ATTACKS, AND HOW DID
YOU HANDLE THE UNCERTAINTY?

"We are living in a revolutionary, changing time. None of us will ever
be the same. Look at all the fear generated with this anthrax problem
in the last few days. People are afraid. Man's moral ability has lagged
behind the technological. The greatest need in the world is human
transformation. . . . We're living right now in history where I wouldn't
want to live for the next five years if I knew I didn't know Christ."

—*ASHEVILLE CITIZEN-TIMES,* OCTOBER 13, 2001

WHAT WAS YOUR POLITICAL STANCE JUST AFTER THE 9/11
TERRORIST ATTACKS, AND WERE YOU AFRAID TO PREACH IN A
PLACE THAT MIGHT BE ANOTHER TERRORIST TARGET?

"I'm not going to get involved in all the political things or even the
war, except to refer to it in the context that we are in a different kind
of war that may involve us in the future. . . . This [the stadium] will
be the safest place you can go. If you have that many people and the
Lord here, there's not going to be any trouble here."

—THE ASSOCIATED PRESS STATE, OCTOBER 9, 2001, ON THE CENTRAL VALLEY
CRUSADE HELD AT CALIFORNIA STATE UNIVERSITY, FRESNO

AFTER THE 9/11 ATTACKS, MANY AMERICANS BLAMED MUSLIMS
OR THE RELIGION OF ISLAM FOR THE ATTACKS. WHAT WAS
YOUR RESPONSE?

"I certainly can't say that God did it or that God judged us. I can't say
the Muslim people did it. They didn't."

— *THE WASHINGTON TIMES*, OCTOBER 8, 2001

IS THERE ANY WAY TO DEFEAT TERRORISM?

"We're facing a new kind of enemy. We're involved in a new kind of
warfare and we need the help of the spirit of God."

— *PRESS JOURNAL* (VERO BEACH, FL), SEPTEMBER 30, 2001

AS A NATION, WHAT SHOULD HAVE BEEN THE UNITED STATES'
RESPONSE TO THE ATTACKS ON 9/11?

"Yes, our nation has been attacked. But now we have a choice
whether to implode and disintegrate emotionally and spiritually as a
people and a nation, or whether we choose to become stronger
through all of the struggle to rebuild on a solid foundation."

— *CHICAGO TRIBUNE*, SEPTEMBER 16, 2001

WAS IT JUSTIFIED TO BOMB AFGHANISTAN AFTER THE 9/11
ATTACKS?

"There are times we have to defend ourselves. I think the Scriptures
are very clear that we are to defend ourselves if we're attacked. On
9/11, we were attacked. And I think that we have responded to that
attack. And I'm praying we can find a way out of the situation now."

— MSNBC's *SCARBOROUGH COUNTRY*, JUNE 24, 2005

DID ANYTHING POSITIVE COME OUT OF THE 9/11 ATTACKS?
"A tragedy like this could have torn our country apart, but instead it has united us and we've become a family. So those perpetrators who took this on to tear us apart, it has worked the other way. It backfired. We're more united than ever before."

— *THE FLORIDA TIMES-UNION* (JACKSONVILLE), SEPTEMBER 16, 2001

IN YOUR OPINION, COULD OIL BRING ON A WAR?
"Much of the wealth that the West collected and accumulated since World War II is now draining to the oil-producing nations, and this is going to create an imbalance and it's going to be a very dangerous situation because it could bring about war."

— *TULSA WORLD* (OKLAHOMA), OCTOBER 3, 2004

On YOUNG PEOPLE

WHAT GENERAL MESSAGE DO YOU HAVE FOR YOUNG PEOPLE
ABOUT THEIR CHOICES IN LIFE?
"You've reached a crossroads in your life and you're trying to decide
which way to go. . . . You have a feeling of non-belonging or restless-
ness. There's an empty place and you're not quite sure what to do with
it. Deep down inside there's something you have not found yet.
Accept Jesus Christ."

—ASSOCIATED PRESS, OCTOBER 18, 1999

CAN YOUNG PEOPLE FIND SOLACE OUTSIDE OF GOD, PERHAPS
THROUGH WEALTH OR POSSESSIONS?
"They never really find an answer until they find it in God." *(On
young people searching for meaning in life through material and sometimes sinful things)*

—*THE BOSTON GLOBE*, SEPTEMBER 27, 1999

WHY DO YOU THINK THAT YOUNG PEOPLE ARE MORE
RECEPTIVE THAN OLDER FOLKS TO YOUR MESSAGE?
"We in America have lost our bearings. We've lost our way, and
young people are wandering. Many of them feel lost and confused.
We're in sort of an ethical vacuum, it seems to me. We don't know

the answers to give to young people. . . . Our crusades are mostly young people. It seems to me they are much more interested and curious, and will listen to an older man."

— *CHICAGO TRIBUNE*, JUNE 7, 1999

HOW DO YOU COUNTER ASSERTIONS THAT YOUNG PEOPLE DON'T CARE ABOUT WHAT'S GOING ON IN THE WORLD?
"*The New York Times* calls this an indifferent generation. I don't believe that; I think you do care. I think you are a terrific generation. I think this will be the best generation ever."

— *THE INDIANAPOLIS STAR*, JUNE 6, 1999

HOW DO YOU REACH YOUNG PEOPLE WITH YOUR MESSAGE?
"I don't understand their language and they don't understand mine. Contemporary music helps us interpret each other. Young people are looking for something to hold on to. I think we made a terrible mistake when we took God and prayer out of school, and put sex education in."

— COX NEWS SERVICE, JUNE 2, 1999

YOU HAVE DISAGREED WITH THOSE WHO SAY THAT GUNS ARE THE PROBLEM. RATHER, YOU BELIEVE THAT "PEOPLE KILL PEOPLE," ESPECIALLY IN THE CASE OF YOUNG PEOPLE KILLING OTHERS AT COLUMBINE HIGH SCHOOL. RIGHT?
"I have been saddened and deeply moved by the television coverage as this situation has unfolded. I agree with those who have remarked that the problem is not guns—rather the hearts of people which need to be changed. I would add that only God can change our hearts." *(Commenting on the shooting deaths at Columbine High School in Littleton, Colorado)*

— *THE DALLAS MORNING NEWS*, APRIL 24, 1999

DO MANY YOUNG PEOPLE HAVE "HOLES IN THEIR HEARTS"?

"We read in our newspapers about children shooting children—killing children. Whether it's in Arkansas, England or wherever it is, their hearts are searching. There's an empty place. You have everything, except something you're not quite sure what it is. There's a hole in your heart and in your life. You'd like it to be filled, but you don't know what it is. And you've tried so many things, like drugs and sex. All these things haven't satisfied the deepest longing you have because that something you're looking for is God."

—PR NEWSWIRE, JUNE 29, 1998

WHAT ARE YOUNG PEOPLE MISSING IN THEIR LIVES?

"You have everything except something, but you're not quite sure what it is. . . . You've tried drugs maybe, you've tried sex but it hasn't stopped this deepest longing. That something is God—God made you in his image. He loves you and sent his son Jesus Christ to die for you."

—*THE OTTAWA SUN*, JUNE 28, 1998

HOW HAS MUSIC HELPED YOU REACH YOUNG PEOPLE DURING YOUR CRUSADES?

"I don't understand the music. I don't understand the words. But at the end when they put their arms around me and hug me, I think the young people know that [the Christian rock bands] accept me and they want to hear what I have to say."

—*ST. PETERSBURG TIMES* (FLORIDA), OCTOBER 21, 1998

WHAT ADVICE DO YOU GIVE TO COLLEGE GRADUATES JUST STARTING THEIR ADULT LIVES?

"I urge each of you to invest your lives, not just spend them. Each of us is given the exact same amount of seconds, minutes, and hours per day as anyone else. The difference is how we redeem our allotted time. . . . You cannot count your days, but you can make your days count."

—COMMENCEMENT ADDRESS TO PALM BEACH
ATLANTIC COLLEGE, *THE LEDGER* (LAKELAND, FL), MAY 16, 1997

WHAT WAS YOUR REACTION TO TAKING RELIGION OUT OF
PUBLIC SCHOOLS?
"We can't hang up the Ten Commandments in the classroom. We're throwing God out and bringing sex in, and look what has happened."

—SPEAKING BEFORE A JOINT SESSION OF THE NORTH CAROLINA
LEGISLATURE, *THE NEWS AND OBSERVER* (RALEIGH, NC), MAY 6, 1997

WHAT HAVE YOU TOLD YOUNG PEOPLE ABOUT THE
UNCERTAINTY AND BREVITY OF THEIR LIVES?
"In a few minutes, you'll have a diploma in your hand and you'll have a life of uncertain length ahead of you. For some of you it will be wonderfully long, and for others it will be surprisingly short. And if you reach my age, you will wonder where time has gone."

—COMMENCEMENT ADDRESS AT LIBERTY UNIVERSITY,
ASSOCIATED PRESS, MAY 5, 1997

From the same commencement address:
"People are the stocks into which we are to invest our time. . . . The best of all investments you can make is to help people come to know Jesus as their Lord and Savior. You can make a commitment right here and now. . . . I'm asking you today not to graduate but commence a new life for God every step of the way."

—*RICHMOND TIMES DISPATCH* (VIRGINIA), MAY 4, 1997

YOU'VE SAID THAT THE ROCK OPERA *JESUS CHRIST SUPERSTAR*
HAS ACTUALLY BEEN HELPFUL TO YOUR MISSION. IN WHAT WAY?
"It's causing millions of young people to think about Jesus and ask
some questions about him."

— *THE COMMERCIAL APPEAL* (MEMPHIS), OCTOBER 20, 1996,
CITING AN INTERVIEW IN 1971, WHEN THE SHOW FIRST APPEARED

WHY DO YOU OFTEN STRESS PREACHING TO YOUNG PEOPLE?
"When you have such pluralism and the problems of secularism, and
the grasp humanism has on the thinking of young people . . . my
preaching will primarily be for young people." *(Before preaching at
Toronto's SkyDome)*

— *THE TORONTO SUN*, JUNE 6, 1995

YOU HAVE EXPRESSED CONCERN FOR THE LONELINESS AND
EMPTINESS THAT YOUNG PEOPLE ARE SHOWING. CAN WE BE
LONELY EVEN AMONG OTHER PEOPLE?
"People can be lonely in marriage, in a crowd, in the midst of a dis-
cotheque. We're a lonely people on a lonely planet in a lonely world."

— *CHATTANOOGA TIMES FREE PRESS* (TENNESSEE), JUNE 23, 1995

HAVE YOU BEEN SURPRISED AT HOW ATTENTIVE YOUNG
PEOPLE CAN BE AT YOUR SERMONS?
"I wondered if these same people who listen to the rap music and all
the rest of that would actually listen to a 70-year-old man. But they
did listen all the way. It was quiet enough to hear a pin drop."
(Speaking about a recent mission in Cleveland)

— *THE COLUMBIAN* (VANCOUVER, WA), AUGUST 5, 1994

HOW SHOULD OLDER PEOPLE GUIDE YOUNGER PEOPLE?

"Old men will dream dreams—that means that they will know how to support the vision of the young. It is not easy for an older generation to hand the torch to a new one, but that is what is happening here tonight. I thank God for the young men and women that He has raised up, not only in this seminary but in other parts of the world."

—SPEAKING AT THE INAUGURATION OF DR. R. ALBERT
MOHLER JR., THE NINTH PRESIDENT OF THE SOUTHERN
BAPTIST THEOLOGICAL SEMINARY, PR NEWSWIRE, OCTOBER 15, 1993

UNLIKE MANY ADULTS, YOU DON'T BELIEVE THAT ALL YOUNG PEOPLE ARE GOING TO HELL. WHY ARE YOU SO OPTIMISTIC?

"We have an idea that all young people are going to hell. Well, they're not. Thousands and millions of them are going to heaven because they believe in Christ and trust in Him."

—*PITTSBURGH POST-GAZETTE* (PENNSYLVANIA), JUNE 6, 1993

WHAT DO YOU TELL YOUNG PEOPLE ABOUT THE PRICE THEY PAY FOR SEX OUTSIDE MARRIAGE?

"Your body is the temple of the Holy Spirit. Every part of your body belongs to God, even sex. People sometimes get the idea that sex is wrong. There's nothing wrong with sex; it's the way people sometimes abuse it. You haven't experienced the deepest enjoyment and thrill that sex can be until it is within marriage. There's no such thing as free sex or free love. There's a price you pay with broken relationships and broken lives."

—*NEWSDAY* (NEW YORK), SEPTEMBER 21, 1990

YOU BELIEVE IN THE SEPARATION OF CHURCH AND STATE, BUT
HAVE SCHOOLS GONE TOO FAR?
"School used to be a place where young people learned the difference
between right and wrong. I think sometimes school boards have gone
much farther than the Supreme Court ever dreamed they'd go. They
need to at least talk about morality—youth want to know what's right
and wrong."

—PR NEWSWIRE, SEPTEMBER 25, 1989

IS IT MORE DIFFICULT FOR YOUNG PEOPLE TODAY TO LIVE A
CHRISTIAN LIFE COMPARED TO WHEN YOU WERE YOUNG?
"I think it is more difficult for a young person to live a pure and
Christian life than when I was young. I think they have many more
temptations, they have many more peer pressures, they have a great
deal of access to automobiles, alcohol, drugs, that sort of thing, and a
great deal of wonderful things on television. But there is also a great
deal of pornography on television. They have many more temptations
and avenues of temptations. Many more problems resisting it. I think
only a truly committed young person can really live a pure life today."

— *THE POST-STANDARD* (SYRACUSE, NY), APRIL 25, 1989

DO YOUNG PEOPLE TURN TO DRUGS OUT OF HOPELESSNESS?
"A person can live a lifetime without sex; possibly 75 days without
food; 10 days without water and six minutes without oxygen, but it is
impossible to live very long without hope, which is why young people
are turning to drugs."

—PR NEWSWIRE, SEPTEMBER 21, 1988

WHAT WAS YOUR ADVICE TO ADULTS ABOUT GIVING
TEENAGERS HEROES TO BELIEVE IN?
"Hold out mirrors to young people. Let them see what will happen

. . . if these present moral trends continue. Give these young people a batch of new heroes. There's a hunger in the country."

— SPEAKING ON SPORTS HEROES AT AN ASSOCIATED PRESS LUNCHEON
OF THE AMERICAN NEWSPAPER PUBLISHERS ASSOCIATION
CONVENTION, ASSOCIATED PRESS, MAY 7, 1985

YOU'VE SAID THAT COLLEGE STUDENTS ARE NOT "WILLING TO PAY THE PRICE" OF BEING DEVOUT. WHAT DID YOU MEAN BY THAT?
"They know the biblical ideal comes nearest to what they want, but they don't want to pay the price of being devout Christians or devout Jews. There are moral demands that many students don't want to live up to. There's a wistfulness about them. They want it but they don't want to pay the price."

— ASSOCIATED PRESS, JANUARY 7, 1983

WHAT OTHER ROLES DOES MUSIC PLAY IN REACHING YOUNG PEOPLE DURING YOUR CRUSADES?
"I think that, just as when I go to another country, I have a translator. These young people with their music—music that I don't quite understand—are the translators. They can open the door for me to speak to young people because they know that I love them and I accept them."

— *THE DALLAS MORNING NEWS*, OCTOBER 20, 2002

IN YOUR OPINION, WHAT DO YOUNG PEOPLE WANT MORE THAN ANYTHING ELSE?
"Our youth are looking to be loved, recognized as individuals, accepted, listened to. They want the security, authority, discipline and someone to believe in, to satisfy their hearts."

— *THE NEW YORK POST*, JUNE 26, 2005

BILLY GRAHAM'S
9/11 SPEECH

We come together today to reaffirm our conviction that God cares for us, whatever our ethnic, religious, or political background may be. The Bible says that He's the God of all comfort, who comforts us in our troubles. No matter how hard we try, words simply cannot express the horror, the shock, and the revulsion we all feel over what took place in this nation on Tuesday morning.

September 11 will go down in our history as a day to remember. Today we say to those who masterminded this cruel plot and to those who carried it out that the spirit of this nation will not be defeated by their twisted and diabolical schemes. Someday, those responsible will be brought to justice, as President Bush and our Congress have so forcefully stated.

But today we especially come together in this service to confess our need of God. We've always needed God, from the very beginning of this nation, but today we need Him especially. We're facing a new kind of enemy, we're involved in a new kind of warfare, and we need the help of the spirit of God.

The Bible's words are our hope. "God is our refuge and strength, an ever present help in trouble. Therefore we will not fear, though the earth give way and the mountains fall into the heart of the sea."

But how do we understand something like this? Why does God allow evil like this to take place? Perhaps that is what you are asking now. You may even be angry at God. I want to assure you that God understands these feelings that you may have. We've seen so much on our television and on our—heard on our radio—stories that bring tears to our eyes and make us all feel a sense of anger. But God can be trusted, even when life seems at its darkest.

But what are some of the—but what are some of the lessons we can learn? First, we are reminded of the mystery and reality of evil. I've been asked hundreds of times in my life why God allows tragedy and suffering. I have to confess that I really do not know the answer totally, even to my own satisfaction. I have to accept by faith that God is sovereign and He's a God of love and mercy and compassion in the midst of suffering.

The Bible says that God is not the author of evil. It speaks of evil as a mystery. In 1 Thessalonians 2:7, it talks about the mystery of iniquity. The Old Testament prophet Jeremiah said, "The heart is deceitful above all things and beyond cure. Who can understand it?" He asked that question, "Who can understand it?" And that's one reason we each need God in our lives.

The lesson of this event is not only about the mystery of iniquity and evil, but secondly, it's a lesson about our need for each other. What an example New York and Washington have been to the world these past few days. None of us will ever forget the pictures of our courageous firefighters and police, many of whom have lost friends and colleagues, or the hundreds of people attending— or standing patiently in line to donate blood. A tragedy like this could have torn our country apart, but instead it has united us, and we have become a family.

So those perpetrators who took this on to tear us apart—it has worked the other way; it's backlash—it's backfired; we are more united than ever before. I think this was exemplified in a very moving way when the members of our Congress stood shoulder to shoulder the other day and sang "God Bless America."

Finally, difficult as it may be for us to see right now, this event can give a message of hope—hope for the present and hope for the future. Yes, there is hope. There's hope for the present, because I believe the stage has already been set for a new spirit in our nation. One of the things we desperately need is a spiritual renewal in this country. We need a spiritual revival in America, and God has told us in His Word time after time that we're to repent of our sins and return to Him, and He will bless us in a new way.

But there's also hope for the future because of God's promises. As a Christian, I have hope, not just for this life, but for heaven and the life to come. And many of those people who died this past week are in heaven right now, and they wouldn't want to come back. It's so glorious and so wonderful. And that's the hope for all of us who put our faith in God.

I pray that you will have this hope in your heart. This event reminds us of the brevity and the uncertainty of life. We never know when we, too, will be called into eternity. I doubt if even one of those people who got on those planes or walked into the World Trade Center or the Pentagon last Tuesday morning thought it would be the last day of their lives. They didn't—it didn't occur to them, and that's why each of us needs to face our own spiritual need and commit ourselves to God and His will now.

Here in this majestic National Cathedral, we see all around us symbols of the cross. For the Christian—I'm speaking for the Christian now—the cross tells us that God understands our sin and our suffering, for He took upon Himself, in the person of Jesus Christ, our sins and our suffering. And from the cross God declares, "I love you. I know the heartaches and the sorrows and the pains that you feel, but I love you." The story does not end with the cross, for Easter points us beyond the tragedy of the cross to the empty tomb. It tells us that there is hope for eternal life, for Christ has conquered evil and death and hell.

Yes, there is hope. I've become an old man now, and I've

preached all over the world. And the older I get, the more I cling to that hope that I started with many years ago and began—and proclaimed it in many languages to many parts of the world.

Several years ago at the National Prayer Breakfast here in Washington, Ambassador Andrew Lu-Young, who had just gone through the tragic death of his wife, closed his talk with a quote from the old hymn "How Firm a Foundation." We all watched in horror as planes crashed into the—the steel and glass of the World Trade Center. Those majestic towers, built on solid foundations, were examples of the prosperity and creativity of America. When damaged, those buildings eventually plummeted to the ground, imploding in upon themselves. Yet underneath the debris is a foundation that was not destroyed. Therein lies the truth of that old hymn that Andrew Young quoted, "How Firm a Foundation."

Yes, our nation has been attacked, buildings destroyed, lives lost, but now we have a choice—whether to implode and disintegrate emotionally and spiritually as a people and a nation, or whether we choose to become stronger through all of the struggle to rebuild on a solid foundation. And I believe that we're in the process of starting to rebuild on that foundation. That foundation is our trust in God. That's what this service is all about, and in that faith we have the strength to endure something as difficult and horrendous as what we've experienced this week.

This has been a terrible week, with many tears, but also it's been a week of great faith. Churches all across the country have called prayer meetings. And today is a day that they're celebrating, not only in this country, but in many parts of the world. And in the words of that familiar hymn that Andrew Young quoted, it says, "Fear not. I am with thee. Oh, be not dismayed for I am thy God and will give thee aid. I'll strengthen thee, help thee and cause thee to stand upon my righteous—on thy righteous, omnipotent hand."

My prayer today is that we will feel the loving arms of God wrapped around us and will know in our hearts that He will never forsake us as we trust in Him. We also know that God is going to give wisdom and courage and strength to the president and those around him. And this is going to be a day that we will remember as a day of victory.

May God bless you all.

OTHER THOUGHTS
and IDEAS

AFTER THE ATTEMPTED ASSASSINATION OF POPE JOHN PAUL II,
YOU CALLED THE INCIDENT "A TRAGIC ILLUSTRATION OF THE
MORAL AND SPIRITUAL CHAOS WHICH INFECTS OUR WORLD."
WHAT DID YOU SAY ABOUT THE POPE THAT MOST PEOPLE DID
NOT KNOW?

"His burden and his work for world peace have been far greater than
most people realize . . . the shooting forcefully reminds us of the need
for spiritual renewal in the world."

—UNITED PRESS INTERNATIONAL, MAY 14, 1981

WHAT DOES IT TAKE FOR US TO REALLY APPRECIATE LIFE?

"We cannot truly face life until we have learned to face the fact that
it will be taken away from us."

— *THE RECORD* (KITCHENER-WATERLOO, ONTARIO), JUNE 30, 2000

DID YOU TAKE QUICKLY TO COMPUTERS?

"I have made some advances. I have learned to turn my computer on.
That's about as far as I've gotten."

— *CHICAGO TRIBUNE*, DECEMBER 17, 1999

DID YOU BELIEVE THAT THE YEAR 2000 MEANT THE END OF
TIME, AS SOME PEOPLE THOUGHT?
"There are some who say it's going to be the end of the world, and
some are even putting up water. I don't believe it. It will only come
to an end when God says so."

—ASSOCIATED PRESS, OCTOBER 15, 1999

YOU DELIVERED A PRAYER FOR THE SPECIAL OLYMPICS
CONTENDERS AT CARTER-FINLEY STADIUM IN RALEIGH. WHAT
WAS THAT PRAYER?
"We remember in reading the Bible how often sports are mentioned as illustrators of our spiritual lives. May each participant not
only do their best physically but also be at their best morally and
spiritually."

—ASSOCIATED PRESS, JUNE 26, 1999

THERE ARE LESSONS FROM THE WORLD OF SPORTS THAT CAN
BE TRANSFERRED TO OUR DAILY LIVES, SUCH AS OPERATING
BY RULES, SETTING GOALS, AND THE NEED FOR DISCIPLINE.
BUT WHAT DID YOU SAY TO PEOPLE WHO CARRY THIS
ANALOGY TOO FAR?
"Life is not a practice round where no score is kept. It's serious
business."

—*THE INDIANAPOLIS STAR,* JUNE 7, 1999

DO PETS GET INTO HEAVEN?
"God will prepare everything for our perfect happiness in heaven,
and if it takes my dog being there, I believe he'll be there."

—*THE PHILADELPHIA INQUIRER,* FEBRUARY 7, 1999

WHAT DO YOU CONSIDER THE MOST EVIL DRUG TODAY?

"Alcohol is the worst drug we have today. It alters the thinking of your mind. In the United States, they are trying to ban cigarettes but we never hear a word about banning alcohol. They said Prohibition didn't work. Well, I lived through that and it did work compared to what's going on now."

— *THE OTTAWA SUN*, JUNE 27, 1998

WHAT IS LACKING IN OUR CHURCHES?

"In our churches we have talked about everything but the Bible and people are hungry to know the Bible. We buy Bibles but we don't read them; those that read them don't study them; and we've become rather ignorant when it comes to the teachings of the Word of God. But people are hungry to know the Bible itself and what its message is."

— *THE RECORD* (KITCHENER-WATERLOO, ONTARIO), JUNE 24, 1998

WHAT IS YOUR POSITION ON ABORTION?

"I am against abortion. I think that life is sacred and we should take a position of being against abortion. I think it is wrong to take human life. I think that human life starts at conception."

— PR NEWSWIRE, APRIL 1, 1997

DO YOU BELIEVE THERE MAY BE LIFE ON OTHER PLANETS?

"I can't imagine that we're the only one that has life. That would be a terribly egotistical thing for us to say as a planet. Because I think there is life on other planets. And I believe that God is the god over all of it. That is why he is so awesome and so tremendous. . . . I don't think I can make it [to another planet]. I'd love to, but I don't think NASA has called me to be an astronaut. And if I get there, I don't think I could speak their language, whoever they are."

— *THE DALLAS MORNING NEWS*, OCTOBER 12, 1996

YOU DID NOT SEE THE OLIVER STONE MOVIE ABOUT YOUR
FRIEND RICHARD NIXON BECAUSE YOU THOUGHT IT MIGHT
NOT PORTRAY HIM ACCURATELY. IS THAT RIGHT?
"I was with the Nixons in both the peaks and valleys of their lives.
The Richard and Pat Nixon that I knew served their country with
dedication and distinction for over half a century. I want to remember
them as they really were. . . . I deeply regret the tendency today
to distort the facts and demean the character of outstanding persons
from the past, all in the name of entertainment."

— *THE TIMES-PICAYUNE* (NEW ORLEANS, LA), DECEMBER 28, 1995

CAN WE LEARN ANYTHING FROM POLARIZING EVENTS SUCH AS
THE O. J. SIMPSON MURDER TRIAL?
"Situations like this can force us to ask the important questions in
life, evaluate our priorities and realize how quickly our lives can
change. We need to resolve to do whatever we can, in our own lives
and in our communities, to put a stop to violence—not to glorify it."

— PR NEWSWIRE, OCTOBER 16, 1995

HAS PRAYER HELPED YOUR GOLF GAME?
"I'm afraid golf is one place where God doesn't answer my prayers."

— *LOS ANGELES TIMES*, AUGUST 4, 1995

YOU'VE CHIDED THE NEWS MEDIA FOR ITS COVERAGE OF
RELIGION, SAYING THAT THEY COVER PROFESSIONAL SPORTS
MORE EVEN THOUGH MORE PEOPLE ATTEND CHURCH THAN GO
TO SPORTING EVENTS. WHAT STATISTICS DID YOU PRESENT THEM?
"In any given week, 42 percent of Americans attend at least one religious
service. Someone has pointed out that this is more than attend
all professional baseball games in an entire year."

— *CHARLESTON DAILY MAIL* (WEST VIRGINIA), APRIL 16, 1994, CITING A SPEECH
TO THE AMERICAN SOCIETY OF NEWSPAPER EDITORS IN WASHINGTON, DC

HOW DO YOU THINK MOST PROTESTANTS FEEL ABOUT THE POPE?
"The infallibility of the pope is something Protestants can never accept, but I have a great deal of admiration for the pope, even though I don't accept all his theology. I don't think the differences are important as far as personal salvation is concerned."

— *PLAIN DEALER* (CLEVELAND, OH), MARCH 27, 1994

YOU HAVE BEEN CRITICAL OF SOME TV TALK SHOWS. WHY?
"Many people are watching talk shows, and many of them talk about anything you can think of. Many people get their advice and counsel not from a psychiatrist or psychologist or minister, they get it from those talk shows. That bothers me because they're having a great impact on a lot of people."

—ASSOCIATED PRESS, APRIL 30, 1994

YOU'VE SAID THAT SOME REPORTERS WHO COVER RELIGION DON'T KNOW THE DIFFERENCES BETWEEN VARIOUS DENOMINATIONS OR EVEN WHAT AN EVANGELIST IS. HOW HAS THAT AFFECTED THEIR COVERAGE?
"They did their best and they were honest, but I think they needed more training, they needed more understanding of what they're writing about. . . . I've had several people tell me they don't know where to turn to get a religious editor for their paper. I've had them ask me for recommendations. It's hard for me to find them."

— *EDITOR & PUBLISHER* MAGAZINE, APRIL 30, 1994

IF THERE WAS ONLY ONE PERSON IN TODAY'S WORLD THAT YOU COULD BRING TO CHRIST, WHO WOULD IT BE AND WHY?
"Every person is important to the Lord. I don't think any person is more important than another person in God's sight. Just everybody.

Anyone that the Lord has spoken to and convicted of their sins and need of Christ—I would like to see come to Christ."

—IN ANSWER TO AN ONLINE QUESTION POSED DURING AN HOUR-LONG GUEST APPEARANCE ON AMERICA ONLINE. *LOS ANGELES TIMES*, NOVEMBER 27, 1993

ARE WE SOMETIMES TOO NARROWLY FOCUSED IN OUR VIEWS ABOUT THE WORLD?

"Our world today desperately needs people of vision. It is far too easy for any of us to become involved in a narrow self-centered way in the pursuit of our own little goals and to forget that we have a larger obligation, an obligation to serve our neighbor."

—PR NEWSWIRE, JUNE 23, 1992

WHY DOES GOD BRING ON NATURAL DISASTERS?

"I think we have to recognize that God is a god of love and he doesn't allow a thing like this to happen without a purpose. I don't know what the purpose is. It's a mystery to me. I've never figured out all these disasters from the biblical point of view." *(After visiting a muddy tent encampment of earthquake victims in Watsonville, California)*

—ASSOCIATED PRESS, OCTOBER 24, 1989

YOU HAVE DEVOTED AN ENTIRE SERMON DURING AN EIGHT-DAY ARKANSAS CRUSADE TO DRUG ADDICTION. IN YOUR OPINION, IS PUTTING DRUG ADDICTS IN JAIL AND SENDING DRUG ADDICTS TO REHABILITATION A VIABLE SOLUTION?

"Drug abuse is an undisciplined flight from reality, not from something good, but from something evil. Jailing drug dealers and detoxifying drug addicts does not get at the heart and soul of the problem, which is spiritual. . . . The Gospel is the answer to the drug problem, because it alone delivers us. . . . Christ can help you not only in your recovery but in the training period, in your treatment period."

—ASSOCIATED PRESS, OCTOBER 12, 1989;

ARKANSAS DEMOCRAT-GAZETTE (LITTLE ROCK), SEPTEMBER 20, 1989

WHAT IS YOUR OPINION OF THE MOVIE *THE LAST TEMPTATION OF CHRIST*?
"I do not plan to see the film but will not take overt boycotting action by demonstrating in front of a theater that may be showing it. I don't have to see a rape in order to condemn rape. I don't have to see a murder in order to condemn murder. From what I have read, this film is sacrilegious."

—*LOS ANGELES TIMES*, SEPTEMBER 17, 1988

WHAT IS YOUR STANCE ON THE HUMANIST MOVEMENT, WHICH BELIEVES IN A NONRELIGIOUS APPROACH TO SOLVING SOCIAL PROBLEMS?
"I respect the humanists' rights to look at problems differently than I do. And I believe in many of the things they say and do . . . but it's only through religion that man can achieve spiritual fulfillment and live in harmony."

—ASSOCIATED PRESS, JULY 30, 1988, AND

THE POST-STANDARD (SYRACUSE, NY), JULY 30, 1988

ARE SOME THINGS CONSTANT?
"Some things change, some things never change. God never changes. Human nature never changes."

—SPEAKING TO A CROWD AT THE SEVENTEENTH-CENTURY

CHURCH OF OUR LADY OF KAZAN AT KOLOMENSKOYE IN

SOUTHERN MOSCOW, ASSOCIATED PRESS, JUNE 11, 1988

HOW DO YOU VIEW THE ROLE OF SPORTS IN OUR SOCIETY?
"The pluses outweigh the minuses, because I'd rather we put our energies into sports. The only thing that bothers me is the drug problem and the fact that sports have become such a big business. This could cause a game to cease to be a sport, and so one can see danger signals."

—*LOS ANGELES TIMES*, JUNE 17, 1986

WILL STRONG EMOTIONS ABOUT THE HORRORS AND HATREDS ASSOCIATED WITH EVENTS LIKE THE HOLOCAUST EVER DISAPPEAR?
"I think that time will someday come, but it may be too early and the wounds were too deep, and it was such a horrible experience."

—ASSOCIATED PRESS, MAY 1, 1985

YOU'VE OFTEN SAID THAT WE CAN BE LONELY NO MATTER WHERE WE LIVE. WHAT'S THE SOLUTION?
"The number one problem in our world is alienation—rich versus poor, black versus white, labor versus management, conservative versus liberal, east versus west. . . . But Christ came to bring about reconciliation and peace."

—*THE WASHINGTON POST*, MAY 1, 1985

DO YOU HAVE CONCERNS ABOUT GENETIC ENGINEERING?
"The problem with technology today is its misuse. The world has poverty as never before. Genetic engineering frightens me more than the atomic bomb. I even hear they've built a super rat."

—UNITED PRESS INTERNATIONAL, MAY 16, 1983

As a National Safety Council board member, you saw a spiritual link between a person's faith and his or her practice of good driving skills. Can you explain that? "Selfishness, anger, carelessness, neglect, pride, are all symptoms of a deep-rooted cause of a spiritual disease that the Bible calls sin. Accidents, injuries, and fatalities are only the results. . . . Most people do not associate careful and safe driving with spiritual living, but there is a definite connection. . . . I urge all who share in the love of God to show that love by placing life above inconvenience, ego, a self will, impatience and pride. Join me in a covenant both to use safety belts and to protect children in child safety seats each time we use our cars. Let us by example and exhortation show others the nature of our commitment, our belief in the preservation of the whole person. . . .

"The commandment 'Thou shalt not kill' applies to our behavior on the highways as well as to our interpersonal relationships. Join me in a covenant both to use safety belts and to protect children in child safety seats each time we use our cars."

One of the prayers Graham suggested was: "O Lord, Creator, leader of all mankind . . . help me to remember that when I am in my automobile, I am my brother's keeper. Let me find the daily strength to insist my fellow passengers protect themselves in safety belts when they are traveling in the car with me. Let me not waver in my obligation to insist that all infants and toddlers who ride in my car are properly secured." *(Messages prepared for the Safety Sabbath, an effort by the National Safety Council and The National Highway Traffic Safety Administration to ask churches and synagogues to designate the weekend of February 13–14 as "National Safety Sabbath" for all Americans to join in "a religious fellowship to rediscover the safety belt.")*

—United Press International, February 2, 1982:

The Washington Post, January 29, 1982

WHAT ARE YOUR VIEWS ON BIRTH CONTROL?

"I don't see anything in the scriptures that says there's anything wrong with birth control." *(Speaking at the National Press Club)*

— *THE WASHINGTON POST,* MARCH 24, 1979

HOW DID YOU CHARACTERIZE THE FIREFIGHTERS WHO RISKED THEIR LIVES SAVING PEOPLE AT THE WORLD TRADE CENTER AFTER IT WAS ATTACKED ON 9/11?

"Now we know what true heroes are. They're ordinary people like you and me who have done extraordinary things. They laid their lives down for total strangers. This reminds us of what Jesus did for us."

— *ASHEVILLE CITIZEN-TIMES,* OCTOBER 12, 2001

WHEN YOU SHOW COURAGE, DOES THAT SPUR OTHERS TO BE COURAGEOUS?

"Courage is contagious. When a brave man takes a stand, the spines of others are stiffened."

— *CHATTANOOGA TIMES FREE PRESS* (TENNESSEE), JUNE 24, 2001

WHAT IS HELL LIKE?

"I believe that hell is essentially separation from God. That we are separated from God, so we can have hell in this life and hell in the life to come. But to describe hell in vivid terms like I might have done 30 or 40 years ago, I'm not at liberty to do that because whether there is actually fire in hell or not, I do not know."

— *THE TIMES-PICAYUNE* (NEW ORLEANS, LA), JULY 13, 2002, CITING A 1991 COMMENT

WHAT PROMPTED YOU TO START THE DOCUMENTARY FILM COMPANY WORLD WIDE PICTURES ABOUT FIFTY YEARS AGO?

"I recognized the fact that not everyone would respond to the Gospel as the result of coming to a stadium to hear me preach."

— CANADA NEWSWIRE, MAY 29, 2002

WHEN YOU WERE IN LOS ANGELES, YOU MENTIONED THAT IT
COULD BE A MODEL FOR THE REST OF THE NATION BECAUSE
OF THE ETHNIC DIVERSITY. WHAT DID YOU MEAN?
"A few years ago there was a movement in this country called the
Jesus movement, among young people. It would be great if we could
move in that direction now. So much of our culture comes from this
part of the country. We could start another culture with Jesus at the
center, and obeying His commandments. . . . Wouldn't it be wonderful here if this could be a model of racial understanding, right in
Southern California. I see a couple of two different ethnic backgrounds hugging each other—that may be the first time they've done
that. Let's be a generation of huggers."

—PR NEWSWIRE US, NOVEMBER 22, 2004

THE WAR IN IRAQ HAS DRAWN OUR ATTENTION TO THAT
COUNTRY. WHAT IS THE IMPORTANCE OF THAT COUNTRY TO
SCRIPTURE?
"When you look at Iraq, you'll be amazed to find out how much
more of the Bible was there than in the Holy Land. It's a Bible coun-
try as far as history is concerned. The Garden of Eden was there.
Adam and Eve were there."

—*OTTAWA CITIZEN*, NOVEMBER 20, 2004

DID *THE PASSION OF THE CHRIST* HELP PEOPLE TO
UNDERSTAND JESUS CHRIST BETTER?
"In spite of the number seeing the film, many didn't understand the
deeper meaning of the cross. The choice you make tonight will make
your whole life, and it will affect eternity. Where will you be 100 years
from now? You won't be here. The cross guarantees a future life."

—*CHICAGO TRIBUNE*, NOVEMBER 19, 2004

DURING YOUR FIRST MAJOR CRUSADE IN LOS ANGELES, PUBLISHER WILLIAM RANDOLPH HEARST ORDERED HIS REPORTERS ON THE *LOS ANGELES EXAMINER* AND *LOS ANGELES HERALD-EXPRESS* TO "PUFF GRAHAM," IN OTHER WORDS, TO WRITE LAUDATORY PIECES ABOUT YOU. THIS HELPED LAUNCH YOUR CAREER. DID YOU EVER SAY ANYTHING TO HIM?

"I never met [Hearst] and I never corresponded with him. I should have written him and thanked him, but I didn't do that in those days."

— *LOS ANGELES TIMES*, NOVEMBER 17, 2004

HOLLYWOOD PUTS MILLIONS OF DOLLARS INTO CREATING PRETEND RELIGIONS, LIKE *STAR WARS* AND THE FORCE AND *LORD OF THE RINGS*. DO YOU THINK THAT IT'S TRYING TO SATISFY PEOPLE'S NEED FOR SPIRITUALITY?

"Yes. I think there is a spirit—there is a longing in people's minds and hearts for purpose and meaning in their lives. And I think that *Lord of the Rings*, for example, was very much in that direction. I think *Star Wars* too."

— MSNBC's *HARDBALL*, JUNE 27, 2005

DO YOU SAY A SPECIAL PRAYER FOR NEW YORK CITY?

"New York City isn't only a cross-section of the world's population. It is also a cross-section of the world's problems. The Gospel of Christ is the answer—not part of the answer, but the whole answer. . . . I pray for New York. I've been praying for New York since my 20s."

— *THE NEW YORK SUN*, JUNE 22, 2005

WERE YOU SURPRISED WHEN YOU RECEIVED THE 2006
GEORGE BUSH AWARD FOR EXCELLENCE IN PUBLIC SERVICE?
"To be honest, when you first contacted me about this award, I was very
reluctant to accept it. The words 'public service' usually bring to mind
someone who has been active in government or politics, or perhaps a
business leader or philanthropist. But that has not been my calling."

—TO FORMER PRESIDENT GEORGE H. W. BUSH,
THE WASHINGTON TIMES, APRIL 12, 2006

YOU WENT TO NEW ORLEANS AFTER THE DEVASTATION OF
HURRICANE KATRINA. WHAT WERE YOUR IMPRESSIONS OF THE
CITY AFTER THE DISASTER?
"Absolutely overwhelmed. In fact, I couldn't even talk about it after-
ward. I didn't even call my wife to tell her about it. I didn't have the
emotions to convey it to her. I think they should bring every con-
gressman down here to look at it."

—*ASHEVILLE CITIZEN-TIMES* (NORTH CAROLINA), MARCH 10, 2006

What Others Say
about Billy Graham

WIFE, RUTH GRAHAM:

"I'm glad I didn't know what was involved in marrying him. I wouldn't have had the nerve. . . . His Parkinson's disease is no joke. He's suddenly grown into an old man. But there's a silver lining. Along with it, there's sweetness and gentleness."

— *THE TAMPA TRIBUNE* (FLORIDA), OCTOBER 23, 1998

IRENE McMANUS, WHO KNEW BILLY GRAHAM AS A YOUNG STUDENT:

"He'd preach to anything. When we were at the Florida Bible Institute in Temple Terrace, Billy would preach to the birds along the Hillsborough River just for practice. . . . I've never met a man so brilliant, so different. Even when he was 18, he had this unusual talent. He loves the Lord; he loves the people."

—THE ASSOCIATED PRESS STATE & LOCAL WIRE, OCTOBER 22, 1998

SON FRANKLIN GRAHAM:

"I can't replace my father. He is an unusually gifted man that comes by once in a century. I can take the ministry and continue leading people to Christ in my own way. . . . Our styles are different because

we're from a different generation. But the message is no different. . . .
It is about helping people with their relationship with God."

— *ST. PETERSBURG TIMES* (FLORIDA), OCTOBER 11, 1998

"I am not waiting here for something to happen to Daddy so I can
jump in. The day I have to take over for my father will be one of the
saddest days of my life."

— *THE ATLANTA JOURNAL AND CONSTITUTION*, MAY 18, 1996

"I've never known a time when my father had the door locked.
Maybe people think he was kind of a religious zealot or something.
But he's just a normal man. He never tried to push Christianity on us
children. He just set the example at home. What he preached in big
stadiums like this, he preached at home."

— *THE POST-STANDARD* (SYRACUSE, NY), APRIL 29, 1989

WILLIAM MARTIN, AUTHOR OF THE 1991 BIOGRAPHY OF
GRAHAM TITLED *A PROPHET WITH HONOR*:
"Whatever you think of his theology, Billy Graham is one of the
major religious figures of the 20th century by any standard. . . . In his
early days, his appeal was simply that he was an arresting speaker.
Today, many people listen to him because he's Billy Graham, the
greatest evangelist of the 20th century."

— *SAN ANTONIO EXPRESS-NEWS* (TEXAS), APRIL 2, 1997

"Billy Graham has been unwilling to draw lines that would alienate
other people or rule them out of his circle. Many of the other conservative Christians who are involved in politics are not only willing to
do that; they seem bent on doing that."

—NEWHOUSE NEWS SERVICE, JUNE 22, 2005

"Billy Graham has seldom been out in the front of the parade. But he's almost always been in front of his own constituency, particularly with respect to civil rights, poverty and, in the late '70s and early '80s, calling for nuclear disarmament."

— *NEWSDAY* (NEW YORK), JUNE 19, 2005

"I think Billy Graham's greatest legacy will not be a university or any institutions, but it will be the tens of thousands of little Billy Grahams, itinerant evangelists, not well-educated, but who will do the simple door-to-door sales work of the evangelist."

— *THE HERALD-SUN* (DURHAM, NC), OCTOBER 12, 1991

TONY CAMPOLO, DIRECTOR OF THE EVANGELICAL ASSOCIATION FOR THE PROMOTION OF EDUCATION:
"The most significant factor is this: He was the one man on the scene who was able to bridge the gap between evangelicals and mainline Protestant churches. We don't have anybody like that anymore."

— *THE POST AND COURIER* (CHARLESTON, SC), JUNE 19, 2005

A. LARRY ROSS, DIRECTOR OF PUBLIC RELATIONS FOR THE BILLY GRAHAM EVANGELISTIC ASSOCIATION:
"It's not about eloquence. It's something else. God takes over. Billy has demonstrated that over and over."

— *OTTAWA CITIZEN*, OCTOBER 27, 1997

"The thing that I have observed is there aren't two Billy Grahams. The Billy Graham you would see on television or hear preach in a stadium is the same Billy Graham you would meet with one on one. I think he's been faithful to the calling he's had, and God has honored that faithfulness and blessed his ministry."

— *THE DALLAS MORNING NEWS*, MARCH 15, 1995

"He's really charting new territory. None of the great evangelists of history have preached beyond their mid-60s."

—RELIGION NEWS SERVICE, JUNE 24, 2005

"When he retired, I wondered how it would be. But since then, he says he has a greater peace than ever before. He feels he is where God wanted him to be."

—*USA TODAY*, FEBRUARY 21, 2006

SENATE MAJORITY LEADER BOB DOLE:

"I know I speak for millions around the world in saying that no one will ever preach the word of God better than you and no one will ever preach it with a better partner at his side than Ruth."

—UPON GRAHAM AND HIS WIFE RECEIVING THE CONGRESSIONAL
GOLD MEDAL BEFORE A STANDING-ROOM-ONLY CROWD IN
THE CAPITOL ROTUNDA, *THE WASHINGTON TIMES*, MAY 3, 1996

VICE PRESIDENT AL GORE:

"You have touched the hearts of the American family. Few individuals have left such a lasting imprint on American life."

—AT THE SAME CEREMONY, *STAR TRIBUNE* (MINNEAPOLIS, MN), MAY 3, 1996

NORTH CAROLINA GOVERNOR JIM HUNT:

"Billy Graham is a shining star of hope to millions of people all over the world. He has accomplished so many things, inspired so many people, changed so many lives. His message of hope is still ringing, his legacy is everlasting. Dr. Graham, I am so proud of you; but more, I am thankful for you. We are all grateful to you for the good work you have done here and around the world."

—DURING THE DEDICATION CEREMONY OF THE RENAMED INTERSTATE 240
IN BUNCOMBE COUNTY, NOW THE BILLY GRAHAM FREEWAY, IN ASHEVILLE,

NORTH CAROLINA, ATTENDED BY MORE THAN
FIVE HUNDRED PEOPLE, PR NEWSWIRE, APRIL 25, 1996

COLUMNIST KAYS GARY:

"Billy Graham is just like any other Sunday golfer—except he plays only on weekdays and doesn't use the expletives."

— *THE CHARLOTTE OBSERVER* (NORTH CAROLINA), APRIL 20, 1996, CITING A 1958 COLUMN ON GRAHAM PLAYING GOLF AT CHARLOTTE COUNTRY CLUB

SINGER JOHNNY CASH:

"This is the high point of my year every year. Billy Graham is one of the greatest men I've ever been around. He is what he appears to be."

— *THE CHARLOTTE OBSERVER* (NORTH CAROLINA), SEPTEMBER 30, 1996, AFTER SINGING AT A GRAHAM CRUSADE

REV. JIMMY ALLEN, FORMER HEAD OF THE SOUTHERN BAPTIST CONVENTION:

"He's removed the Elmer Gantry image from evangelism." *(On Graham's squeaky-clean image and financial accountability)*

— *THE MIAMI HERALD*, SEPTEMBER 29, 1996

ROGER PALMS, A WRITER WHO HAS SPENT TWENTY-SIX YEARS COVERING CRUSADES FOR THE BILLY GRAHAM EVANGELISTIC ASSOCIATION'S OFFICIAL MAGAZINE:

"He's consistent and faithful. What you see on the platform is what you see all the time."

— *THE POST AND COURIER* (CHARLESTON, SC), SEPTEMBER 28, 1996

GIGI TCHIVIDJIAN-GRAHAM, THE EVANGELIST'S ELDEST DAUGHTER, AND AUTHOR OF *PASSING IT ON*:

"That's been a difficult role [being Billy Graham's child], because people have expectations. Mom and Dad never put that kind of pressure on us. They never sacrificed us to public opinion."

—SPEAKING WHEN HER SIXTH BOOK OF SPIRITUAL INSPIRATION WAS DEDICATED TO

HER FATHER'S SEVENTY-FIFTH BIRTHDAY AND HER PARENTS' FIFTIETH WEDDING

ANNIVERSARY, *ORANGE COUNTY REGISTER* (CALIFORNIA), NOVEMBER 19, 1993

PRESIDENT BILL CLINTON:

"And I remember, I got a Sunday school teacher in my church—and I was about 11 years old—to take me 50 miles to Little Rock so I could hear a man preach who was trying to live by what he said. And then, I remember, for a good while thereafter, trying to send a little bit of my allowance to the Billy Graham Crusade because of the impression he made on me then."

—SPEAKING AT A PRAYER BREAKFAST, U.S. NEWSWIRE, FEBRUARY 4, 1993

"What an honor it is for me to be here, as a person of faith, with a man I love and whom I have followed. He is about the only person I have ever known whom I have never seen fail to live his faith."

—AT THE NEW YORK CRUSADE IN 2005, *THE WASHINGTON POST*, JUNE 27, 2005

ACTOR/COMEDIAN BOB HOPE:

"I can't stand playing golf with Billy Graham. He cheats. How can you play 18 holes when it only rains on you?"

—*CHICAGO TRIBUNE*, AUGUST 4, 1989

HIGH SCHOOL CLASSMATE DOTTIE ALEXANDER POTTER OF ASHEVILLE, NORTH CAROLINA:

"Billy Graham sat across from me in homeroom. He was so fun-loving and mischievous. I think it's just beautiful what his life has come into now. He's touched so many lives."

—AT SHARON HIGH SCHOOL'S CLASS OF 1936'S FIFTIETH REUNION,

ASSOCIATED PRESS, NOVEMBER 23, 1986

SON NED GRAHAM:

"Since taking on more responsibility in my personal life, we have a more equal footing when we talk. He listens to my advice. I listen to his advice. We've become very, very close."

—ASSOCIATED PRESS, MAY 28, 1985

BRITISH AMBASSADOR SIR CHRISTOPHER MEYER:

"He has preached to more people in live audiences than anyone else in history. His ministry is truly international. Dr. Graham has blazed a trail of Christian commitment marked by tolerance and respect for others." *(On conferring honorary knighthood to Billy Graham)*

—*THE HALIFAX DAILY NEWS* (NOVA SCOTIA), DECEMBER 9, 2001

NORTH CAROLINA STATE SENATOR AARON W. PLYLER:

"I don't think there's another man living today that has done things for humanity like Billy Graham." *(On a resolution to proclaim one day in North Carolina as Billy Graham Day)*

—*THE NEWS AND OBSERVER* (RALEIGH, NC), AUGUST 9, 2001

PRESIDENT GEORGE H. W. BUSH:

"Billy Graham has been a pastor to America's first family for as long as I can remember. All of us who have been privileged to call the White House home have gained strength and a greater sense of purpose with his healing ministry."

—*AUSTIN AMERICAN-STATESMAN* (TEXAS), OCTOBER 18, 2002

"When my soul was troubled, it was Billy I reached out to for advice, for comfort and for prayer. You could say Billy has been the conscience of our nation and, sometimes, of the world. . . . No matter how deep one's faith, sometimes you need the guidance and comfort of a living, breathing human being. For me and so many other Oval Office occupants, that person was Billy Graham, the nation's pastor."

REV. LARRY DAVIS, EXECUTIVE COMMITTEE CO-CHAIRMAN OF THE GREATER CINCINNATI/NORTHERN KENTUCKY BILLY GRAHAM MISSION AND PASTOR OF THE FIRST BAPTIST CHURCH IN COLD SPRING, KENTUCKY:
"If you listen to 25 preachers and one is Billy Graham, he may not be at the top of the list. He may not even make the top 10. Yet, when he preaches, lives are changed. It's not in his eloquence and his ability to put a sermon together. It has to be that God uses this man in a way he does not use other men or women."

—*DAYTON DAILY NEWS* (OHIO), JUNE 23, 2002

LONGTIME FRIEND REV. MEL DIBBLE:
"When Bill gave his life to God as a young boy at an old-time revival in the hills of North Carolina, nobody had any idea of the thousands of miles he would travel. Nobody knew the kings and princes and presidents and thousands of people he would tell the words of the Gospel. But God knew. I'm sure of that. . . . So what's the secret of Billy's success? It is the working of God's spirit in his life."

—*THE CINCINNATI ENQUIRER*, JUNE 23, 2002

REV. BILLY MELVIN, EXECUTIVE DIRECTOR OF THE NATIONAL ASSOCIATION OF EVANGELICALS FROM 1967 TO 1995:
"When Billy Graham can no longer fulfill his own ministry and he's in his grave, it's over. The Billy Graham ministry is over. He'll leave behind his association and his son, Franklin, will run the organization, but nobody is going to take his place."

—*THE COLUMBUS DISPATCH* (OHIO), JUNE 21, 2002

COUNTRY SINGER BARBARA MANDRELL:

"Truly I can only think of two people in my life where you knew it when they were in the building just by their presence. The air would just get exciting and stimulating and electric even if you couldn't see them. Those two people were Johnny Cash and Billy Graham."

— *THE STAR PHOENIX* (SASKATOON, SASKATCHEWAN), SEPTEMBER 13, 2003

REV. THOMAS SAMUEL, A REPRESENTATIVE FROM THE INDIA PENTECOSTAL CHURCH OF GOD, WHO HAS TRANSLATED GRAHAM'S SERMONS INTO MALAYALAM, A LANGUAGE SPOKEN IN THE SOUTHERN INDIAN STATE OF KERALA. SAMUEL HAS SAID THAT GRAHAM IS RELATIVELY EASY TO TRANSLATE BECAUSE OF HIS CLEAR AND SIMPLE WAY OF SPEAKING:

"Billy Graham has a very simple message. That's what's unique about Billy Graham."

— *DAILY OKLAHOMAN* (OKLAHOMA CITY), JUNE 8, 2003

BOB BECKETT, PASTOR OF THE DWELLING PLACE CHURCH IN HEMET, CALIFORNIA:

"He has so stood for integrity and what the ministry means to most of us. He has been clean morally and ethically, and stands for what most of us think Christians should stand for. Even though his ministry went global on television he never used it for personal gain or prominence. He has been careful to make the Gospel and salvation the central issue."

— *PRESS ENTERPRISE* (RIVERSIDE, CA), NOVEMBER 8, 2004

AUTHOR C. S. LEWIS DURING A MEETING IN 1954:

"You have many critics, but I have never met one of your critics who knows you personally."

— *INVESTOR'S BUSINESS DAILY*, NOVEMBER 3, 2004

GRAEME KEITH, A CHARLOTTE, NORTH CAROLINA, BUSINESS
EXECUTIVE AND TREASURER OF THE BILLY GRAHAM
EVANGELISTIC ASSOCIATION:
"For an internationally well-known person, he is the most humble
man I have ever known."

— *THE KANSAS CITY STAR,* OCTOBER 2, 2004

MARSHALL SHELLEY, EDITOR OF *LEADERSHIP JOURNAL:*
"Billy Graham has launched a thousand ships. He has scattered seed
widely. That is going to be his legacy."

— *THE LEDGER* (LAKELAND, FL), AUGUST 8, 2004

JON MEACHAM, EDITOR OF *NEWSWEEK* MAGAZINE, ON HIS
STORY "BILLY GRAHAM: LAST CRUSADE":
"Great preachers and great actors and great politicians all have the
same capacity, I think, which is to convince an audience of the
reality we cannot see ourselves. And there he was, once more,
preaching the Gospel of Christ, as he puts it, and refusing, res-
olutely refusing, to be drawn into the passions and storms of the
moment. He wasn't going to talk about stem cells, wasn't going to
talk about gay marriage, wasn't going to talk about judges. He was
going to talk about Jesus and love, and the Pauline virtues of faith,
hope, and love. And that resonated so strongly. You could—at least
I could feel it as a secular person, or as a journalist, that his
strength and his power was that he was not going to talk about the
things that consume us from hour to hour, but about the things
that should consume us from age to age." *(On Graham's last crusade
in New York City)*

— *THE CHARLIE ROSE SHOW,* JUNE 28, 2005

RICHARD MOUW, PRESIDENT OF FULLER THEOLOGICAL
SEMINARY, A PROMINENT EVANGELICAL SCHOOL IN PASADENA,
CALIFORNIA:

"I think Billy Graham came into public awareness at a time when it
was still possible for a single individual to initiate something new and
become a leading spokesperson. I don't think we'll see a person like
that come along again."

—ASSOCIATED PRESS ONLINE, JUNE 27, 2005

ART BAILEY, WHO HAS BEEN SETTING UP GRAHAM'S MASSIVE
CRUSADES FOR 20 YEARS:

"Our internal joke is that we've been doing the last crusade for 10
years. . . . There are no plans for that [coming back to New York City
after the 2005 crusade]. But God is sovereign. There were no plans
to extend the 1957 crusade."

—RELIGION NEWS SERVICE, JUNE 27, 2005

RANDALL BALMER, PROFESSOR OF AMERICAN RELIGIOUS
HISTORY AT BARNARD COLLEGE, COLUMBIA UNIVERSITY:

"He has become a kind of iconic representation of evangelism in
America. Without a doubt he is the most significant evangelical of
the 20th century. Other leaders of the religious right are polemicists.
Graham was never a polemicist."

—*THE BOSTON GLOBE*, JUNE 25, 2005

MICHAEL CROMARTIE, DIRECTOR OF THE EVANGELICALS IN
CIVIC LIFE PROGRAM AT THE ETHICS AND PUBLIC POLICY
CENTER IN WASHINGTON, DC:

"Before taking the country to war, every president from Harry
Truman to Bill Clinton to George Bush calls Billy Graham, who

comes to the White House, spends the night and prays with the president as he makes these difficult decisions. He's been the pastor to people in power."

— *HARTFORD COURANT* (CONNECTICUT), JUNE 24, 2005

CHRIS ROHRS, PRESIDENT OF THE TELEVISION BUREAU OF ADVERTISING:
"Stations have always liked the Billy Graham specials. It's uplifting programming that's well produced and has a loyal audience."

— *THE HOLLYWOOD REPORTER*, JUNE 24, 2005

REV. FRED BEVERIDGE, PASTOR OF PASCACK BIBLE CHURCH IN HILLSDALE, NEW JERSEY:
"He is a man who is not controversial in unnecessary ways. He has guarded his tongue and placed the emphasis on the grace of the Gospels, and that's what a lot of us respect."

— *THE RECORD* (BERGEN COUNTY, NJ), JUNE 22, 2005

DAVID AIKMAN, FORMER *TIME* MAGAZINE CORRESPONDENT AND AUTHOR OF *GREAT SOULS: SIX WHO CHANGED THE CENTURY*, A 1998 BIOGRAPHY OF MR. GRAHAM AND FIVE OTHER TWENTIETH-CENTURY RELIGIOUS FIGURES:
"Perhaps no other individual in the history of the Western world in modern times has been more tempted by the rewards thrust in front of him by a success-worshipping culture. It is little short of astonishing, especially considering the scandals affecting some evangelists of the 1980s, how entirely Graham avoided any major moral or ethical lapse throughout his career."

— *THE WASHINGTON TIMES*, JUNE 22, 2005

REV. ERIC SWENSSON, PASTOR OF HOLY TRINITY LUTHERAN
CHURCH IN NEW ROCHELLE, NEW YORK:
"As far as American religious figures, he's our pope, emotionally
speaking."

— *THE JOURNAL NEWS* (WESTCHESTER COUNTY, NEW YORK), JUNE 19, 2005

FRED BARNES, COHOST, *THE BELTWAY BOYS*:
"I used to be cynical about Billy Graham and his ministry to leaders
of the country, the presidents and so on. And, you know, after hearing him and knowing more about him, I think it's a great ministry,
and he has served the leaders of the presidents in particular extremely
well. And if I were president and I had some big decision to make,
I'd want his counsel and his prayers."

—FOX NEWS NETWORK'S *THE BELTWAY BOYS*, JUNE 18, 2005

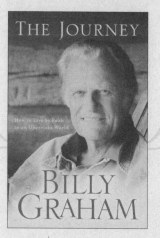

B ILLY GRAHAM is respected and loved around the world. And this work is his magnum opus, the culmination of a lifetime of experience and ministry!

Chapter by chapter, Graham leads us on a journey in faith. We learn about God and his purpose for our lives; who Jesus is and what he has done for us. We learn to deal with challenges along the way: temptation; wrong thoughts and motives, habits that destroy our spirit, and what to do when life turns against us. And we are given practical advice on the Bible, prayer, knowing God's will, making right decisions, finding fellowship, strengthening our marriage, being wise parents, and using our gifts to share Christ with others.

With insight that only comes from a life spent with God, *The Journey* is filled with wisdom, encouragement, hope, and inspiration for anyone who wants to live a happier, more fulfilling life.

Available Now Wherever Books Are Sold

THOMAS NELSON
Since 1798